D1429826

ENCOUNTERS WITH FLYING
HUMANOIDS

About the Author

Ken Gerhard is a cryptozoologist and field researcher for the Centre for Fortean Zoology and Gulf Coast Bigfoot Research Organization, as well as a fellow of the Pangea Institute and consultant for various paranormal groups. He has appeared on *Monster Quest*, *The Real Wolfman*, *Legend Hunters*, *Paranatural*, *Ultimate Encounters*, and *William Shatner's Weird or What?* He currently lectures and exhibits at events across the United States.

To Write to the Author

If you wish to contact the author or would like more information about this book, please write to the author in care of Llewellyn Worldwide, and we will forward your request. Both the author and publisher appreciate hearing from you and learning of your enjoyment of this book and how it has helped you. Llewellyn Worldwide cannot guarantee that every letter written to the author can be answered, but all will be forwarded. Please write to:

Ken Gerhard
℅ Llewellyn Worldwide
2143 Wooddale Drive
Woodbury, MN 55125-2989

Please enclose a self-addressed stamped envelope for reply,
or $1.00 to cover costs. If outside the USA, enclose
an international postal reply coupon.

KEN GERHARD

ENCOUNTERS WITH FLYING HUMANOIDS

mothman, manbirds, gargoyles
& other winged beasts

Llewellyn Publications
Woodbury, Minnesota

FIRST EDITION
First Printing, 2013

Book design by Bob Gaul
Cover illustration by Dominick Finelle/The July Group
Cover design by Kevin R. Brown
Interior photos by Dr. Karl P.N. Shuker, Thomas E. Finley, Jonathan Lackey, Linda S. Godfrey, Ginger Bertline, Ken Gerhard, Frank Ramirez, Jon Huston, and Nick Redfern

Llewellyn Publications is a registered trademark of Llewellyn Worldwide Ltd.

Library of Congress Cataloging-in-Publication Data (Pending)
978-0-7387-3720-1

Llewellyn Publications
A Division of Llewellyn Worldwide Ltd.
2143 Wooddale Drive
Woodbury, MN 55125-2989
www.llewellyn.com

Printed in the United States of America

CONTENTS

FOREWORD

One afternoon during the early 1980s, I was browsing through the upstairs second-hand department of Andromeda Books— the once-celebrated but now long-demised science fiction and fantasy bookshop in Birmingham, England—when I came upon a paperback entitled *Earth's Secret Inhabitants*, which had been published in 1979. Its front cover illustration was extremely eyecatching—a full-color depiction of two feathery-winged humanoids flying through the sky in a scene captured within the hulking silhouette of a bigfoot-type man-beast.

Initially I'd assumed that this book was a sci-fi novel, but then I noticed that its authors were none other than D. Scott Rogo and Jerome Clark—two leading American non-fiction writers specializing in the field of mysterious phenomena.

And when I turned to the back cover, the blurb revealed that its contents featured a wide range of surreal entities that apparently share our planet but have never been scientifically explained—including a veritable phalanx of winged "batmen." Until then, I'd been largely unaware of these aerial apparitions, but after reading about them in Rogo and Clark's book—because, needless to say, I purchased it immediately!—I was totally captivated by their bizarre histories and extraordinary appearances, and from then on I made a point of collecting as much information concerning them as I could find.

The most immediate problem that I have always faced whenever doing so, however, is that such material is extremely disparate, scattered loosely among countless publications, yet rarely compiled or assimilated into any kind of lucid or lengthy coverage. This is why I was delighted to learn recently that Ken Gerhard was writing a book-length treatment of these winged wonders and even more delighted when he very kindly invited me to write a foreword for it.

Reading through his book, *Encounters with Flying Humanoids*, it is evident that Ken shares my own fascination with the batmen and man-birds that have haunted our skies for many centuries, continue to be encountered even today, in all parts of the world, and assume a diverse assortment of forms. Moreover, unlike previous writers, he has not been content to limit his coverage to such perennially chronicled enigmas as Mothman, Owlman, and the man-bats of Texas, but has cast his gaze like a vast skyborne net far and wide through time and space, encompassing many much more obscure examples that even I, despite having spent years of collecting material myself, had never previously heard of.

Consequently, *Encounters with Flying Humanoids* very commandingly fills a sizeable, (all-too-)long-present gap in the Fortean and cryptozoological literature, and it also makes enthralling, if not a little disturbing, reading. What are these mysterious flying figures with plumes of bird or pinions of bat, and where have they originated? Do they truly belong somewhere within our planet's grand scheme of things, or are they visitors from the great beyond— from alien worlds, planes, or dimensions, rarefied realms stranger than we can even begin to suspect? And if so, why are they here? What might their purpose be?

A worthy successor to his previous highly acclaimed volumes on winged mystery beasts and cryptids of Texas, Ken's latest, superb book is a timely reminder of just how outlandish our land can sometimes be, how otherworldly our world may sometimes seem, and that there truly are more things— especially with wings—in heaven and earth, gentle reader, than are dreamt of in anyone's philosophy!

Dr. Karl P.N. Shuker,
Wednesbury, England,
December 2012

"Dr. Karl P.N. Shuker with a friend" © Dr. Karl P.N. Shuker

INTRODUCTION:

Flying Humanoids—
The Manbirds and Other
Incomprehensibles

On a dark and desolate rural road, two young couples are chased at high speed by a terrifying apparition—an unearthly winged entity that defies explanation by our understanding of the natural world. Suddenly and inexplicably, a sleepy West Virginia community is thrust into a vortex of the oddest nature, culminating in a tragic disaster that touches everyone within reach. There are still many who believe that the so-called Mothman that was encountered by dozens of residents during the 1960s was a bad omen, a shadowy portent of destruction, and that its manifestation spelled doom for all who were unfortunate enough to cross its path. Skeptics have since argued that individuals had misidentified a large owl that was lurking in the area and that the rest was merely the product of mass hysteria and overly fanciful imaginations. Yet in many cultures, the appearance of an owl outside someone's window is considered to be a premonition of death . . . a connection perhaps?

Since the dawn of mankind, humans have glanced skyward, dreaming about life among the clouds. Wondering what it would be like to escape our earth-borne existence and soar effortlessly through the air like birds, bats, bugs, and other creatures that have evolved in defiance of gravity. True, men have devised artificial vessels that enable us to break free from the confines of terra firma, allowing us to travel great distances in brief periods of time. But this is not the natural order of things. Without these crafts, we are obliged by both gravity and evolutionary design to remain earthbound, unlike the animals that take to the sky. So then what are we to make of the surprising number of accounts that describe humanlike figures flying freely overhead?

Throughout the course of human history, for thousands of years there has existed a cross-cultural belief in anthropomorphic, sentient beings. They are frequently portrayed as having both human and avian characteristics, specifically wings. These traditions literally span the globe, and the imagery seems familiar to us on many levels. What is truly fascinating is the symbolism of what these demigods seem to represent. While the delineations vary to some extent, there is one overlying and foreboding theme: the notion that these visitors are ominously dangerous and obscene, the essence of evil incarnate. Although their ubiquity in so many ancient mythologies is uncanny, the truth is that they've never really left us, as you shall soon discover.

In the pages that follow, we will examine the perplexing phenomenon of flying humanoids—from West Virginia's weird Mothman to the Angels of Mons and the birdpeople that have been observed stalking both treetops and rooftops around the world. Why is popular belief in these entities so widespread, and why do people in modern times continue to report run-ins with these assorted airborne aberrations? Many theories have been put forward, ranging from misidentifications of enigmatic, giant birds to inter-dimensional origins. So read on if you dare to enter a place where winged gargoyles and flying witches can be seen flitting through our modern skies. I offer you the positively absurd with an assurance that there do appear to be things in the stratosphere that resemble us.

ONE

Dawn of the Twentieth Century: Man Takes Flight

Da Vinci's Ornithopter

Few would argue that one of the most brilliant intellects in human history belonged to the eminent polymath Leonardo da Vinci. A superlative artist, scientist, and visionary, Da Vinci was the epitome of a Renaissance man. Born near Vinci, in Italy's Tuscany region on April 15, 1452, Leonardo studied under some of the great painters of his time and gleaned a great deal from many disciplines, ranging from anatomy and design to chemistry and engineering. He seemed to have an innate ability to diagnose and conceptualize a diverse range of topics and to apply his vast knowledge base and skill set in tangible ways.

One of Da Vinci's more intriguing pursuits was the design and attempted development of several flying machines. His extreme fascination with becoming airborne is evident, based on his treatise *Codex on the Flight of Birds* in which he broke down the aerodynamics that pertain to avians, including their anatomy and wing structure, as well as their dependence on air currents, balance, and gravity in order to achieve flight and maintain control. Though Da Vinci visualized inventions such as the parachute, and even the helicopter, centuries before their creation, it is his designs of so-called ornithopters that are relevant here.

It is apparent from Da Vinci's early paintings of winged angels that he was captivated with the structural morphology of airfoils. He seemed to pay painstaking attention to detail in these early renderings and began to sketch blueprints of artificial wings between the years 1487 and 1490. Initially inspired to develop a pair of mechanical wings that could be guided and controlled by human propulsion, Leonardo soon learned that there were many drawbacks to this particular design, specifically the weight of a man, once bridled with the contraption. Additionally, he had concerns about how a human could adapt to manipulating the appendages while maintaining adequate balance and control. Da Vinci later gravitated to a glider type of design that would allow the pilot to utilize wind currents, while sacrificing flexibility.

For years, there has been an ongoing debate as to whether or not Leonardo ever successfully tested any of his flying machines, though it has been suggested that at one time, he had a plan that involved launching off the roof of a tall building known as the Corte Vecchia. Later in life, his writings indicated that men would be wise to abandon their dreams of flight. But intriguingly, his aerial painting titled *Bird's-Eye View of a Landscape* is so accurate that it causes one to wonder.

Da Vinci was certainly not the first man to contemplate an attempt at flight. History has accounts of others who attached artificial wings to their bodies, jumping off of high perches in an effort to mimic birds. The stories typically end the same way, with the subjects plummeting to their deaths before a crowd of curious onlookers. Subsequently, three centuries after Da Vinci's time, Frenchmen Jean-François Pilâtre de Rozier and François Laurent became the first humans to officially defy gravity when they piloted an unfettered hot air balloon over Paris for twenty minutes on November 21, 1783. At long last, man had fulfilled his dream of flight.

Vespertilio—homo and
the Great Moon Hoax

Fifty-two years after humans first took to the sky, the world was changing. Trains, telegraphs, electromagnets, and even calculators had recently been invented, and in the Western Hemisphere, a young nation was burgeoning. People were clambering to read about new developments and scientific advancements in the daily newspapers. One such publication was the *New York Sun*.

Beginning on August 21, 1835, the *Sun* published a series of six sensational articles that rocked the world. Attributed to the research of renowned English astronomer Sir John Herschel, the essays outlined his alleged discovery of life on the moon with the aid of an enormous, new type of telescope that had been constructed at the Cape of Good Hope in South Africa. The initial article described Herschel's observation of oceans, forests, animals including bison and goats, and precision lines that seemed to indicate artificial structures, such as roads and buildings. The fourth edition contained the most remarkable revelation of all, that Hershel had actually spotted a race of winged humanoids trotting merrily about on the lunar surface. What follows is the descriptive excerpt as first printed in the *New York Sun* on August 25, 1835. The dialogue is attributed to Hershel's assistant, a man named Dr. Arthur Grant:

We counted three parties of these creatures, of twelve, nine, and fifteen in each, walking erect towards a small wood…Certainly they were like human beings, for their wings had now disappeared and their attitude in walking was both erect and dignified…About half of the first party had passed beyond our canvas; but of all the others we had perfectly distinct and deliberate view. They averaged four feet in height, were covered, except on the face, with short and glossy copper-colored hair, and had wings composed of a thin membrane, without hair, lying snugly upon their backs from the top of the shoulders to the calves of their legs. The face, which was of a yellowish color, was an improvement upon that of the large orangutan…so much so that but for their long wings they would look as well on a parade ground as some of the old cockney militia.

The hair of the head was a darker color than that of the body, closely curled but apparently not woolly, and arranged in two circles over the temples of the forehead. Their feet could only be seen as they were alternately lifted in walking; but from what we could see of them in so transient a view they appeared thin and very protuberant at the heel…We could perceive that their wings possessed great expansion and were similar in structure of those of the bat, being a semitransparent membrane expanded in curvilinear divisions by means of straight radii, united at the back by dorsal integuments. But what astonished us most was the circumstance of this membrane being continued from the shoulders to the legs, united all the way down, though gradually decreasing in width. The

> wings seemed completely under the command of voli-
> tion, for those of the creatures whom we saw bathing in
> the water spread them instantly to their full width, waved
> them as ducks do theirs to shake off the water, and then
> as instantly closed them again in a compact form.

Subsequent details revealed that the beings, which had been scientifically classified as Vespertilio-homo (bat-winged man), had apparently constructed massive, sapphire temples and subsisted primarily on fruit. Understandably, the disser-tation created quite an uproar, resulting in the *Sun* breaking new distribution and sales records in the publishing world.

However, within days it was revealed that the entire epi-sode had been a hoax, conceived and executed by a reporter named Richard Locke. There was no such person as Dr. Arthur Grant, and Hershel had not been involved. Upon hearing that the affair had been fabricated for sensational-istic reasons, most people were amused, though there were many who refused to let the matter go and still believed that Vespertilio-homo actually existed. If nothing else, the en-tire exercise serves as a reminder that the notion of winged humanoids was very much a part of the common collective during the mid-ninteenth century.

Spring—heeled Jack

While memories of the Great Moon Hoax were still rever-berating in the Western consciousness, another sensational chain of events was about to unfold. It revolved around one of the most diabolical and fanciful names ever uttered, that of Spring-heeled Jack. Though not endowed with the gift of flight, this ill-famed figure received his name because of his miraculous ability to bound effortlessly through the air over great distances. A sort of urban legend meets supervillain, Jack was generally described as extremely tall, pale, and thin, though possessing great strength and agility. Victims claimed that he typically wore a helmet, flowing black cape, and a white-skinned jumpsuit. Most disturbing was the fact that his eyes glowed red and his fingers evidently terminated in sharp, metallic claws. Not to mention his toxic breath, which reputedly gushed blue flames. His ears were said to be large and pointy.

Spring-heeled Jack was first encountered in October of 1837, when he attacked a young woman named Mary Stevens at a place called Clapham Common in South London. He allegedly ripped at her clothes and kissed her face before her cries for help caused him to flee the scene. The following day, Jack leapt in front of a horse-drawn carriage, causing a crash that injured the driver. It is said that he was laughing diabolically as he bounded over a high fence with ease. When word of the strange assailant hit the streets, mass hysteria broke out around London, and Lord Mayor Sir Jon Cowan organized a vigilance committee in an attempt to capture or curtail the bizarre criminal.

One of the most terrifying encounters involved a young woman named Jane Alsop, who lived in a remote neighborhood called Bear-bind Cottage. One evening in February 1838, Jane heard the doorbell ring violently, and when she peered out at the front gate, she was confronted by a tall, shadowy figure claiming to be a police officer. The man called out to her, "For God's sake, bring me a light, for we have caught Spring-heeled Jack in the lane!" Just as soon as Jane returned with a candle, the individual seized it from her, discarded his cloak, and held the flame up to his face, revealing "hideous and frightful" features and a weird address that included a large helmet and a tight bodysuit that resembled white oilskin.

The *London Times* reported that the man "vomited forth a quantity of blue and white flames from his mouth" and that "his eyes resembled red balls of fire." Jack seized poor Jane and placed her in a headlock and began to rip her gown, but after a valiant struggle, she managed to break free and dash for safety. However, her assailant followed and grabbed her with steely claws that scratched her skin and pulled out some of her hair. Jane was eventually rescued by her sister as her attacker escaped into the murk once again. In the following months, there were other alleged assaults reported to police, including two sisters who claimed that Jack had also accosted them, breathing blue flames into their faces and causing the younger one to collapse in a series of fits.

Events seemed to trail off after a while, but waves of Spring-heeled Jack reappearances would still resurface from time to time. In 1845, Jack was accused of murder when he supposedly drowned a London prostitute in a sewer after spitting flames into her face. The incident took place in broad daylight, and there were many eyewitnesses, according to reports. Then, in 1877, the city of Norfolk, England, was besieged as Jack was observed bounding across the rooftops with unnaturally superhuman finesse. Two years later, Jack appeared suddenly out of the darkness and slapped a sentry who was standing guard duty at the North Camp Barracks in the town of Aldershot. The soldier claimed that he fired his rifle at the apparition, but with apparently no effect. Spring-heeled Jack's last official exhibition was in Liverpool in 1904. His identity has never been resolved.

Astonishingly, as of this writing, there is an exceptionally current encounter that may add to the mystery. On Valentine's Day 2012, a family from Banstead, a suburb of southern London, claimed they may have sighted Spring-heeled Jack as they were traveling home in a taxicab. According to a British website called *Your Local Guardian*, Scott Martin, his wife, and son spotted a shadowy, manlike figure dash across the thoroughfare they were traveling on and leap over a fifteen-foot-tall fence in a fluid motion before disappearing down a steep embankment. The taxi driver was so upset by the incident that he was fearful of driving back alone. Mr. Martin summarized, "All four of us were baffled and voiced our sighting straight away with the same detail. A dark figure with no real features, but fast in movement with an ease of hurdling obstacles I've never seen."

According to Spring-heeled Jack expert Jack Bowman, other sightings have been logged as recently as 1986 in the city of Birmingham. Whatever the strange saga of Spring-heeled Jack may represent, it appears to be ongoing.

Gotham City's
Original Batman

Six decades before a certain Caped Crusader graced the pages of popular comic books, an odd, batlike being was observed sailing through the skies over New York City. Events first came to light in 1877, when a gentleman named W. H. Smith penned a letter to the *New York Sun* describing "a winged human form" that he had spotted flying over Brooklyn on September 18 of that year.

Almost exactly three years later, an article in the *New York Times* dated September 12, 1880, detailed an incident involving scores of eyewitnesses who sighted a similar entity flying over Coney Island:

One day last week a marvelous apparition was seen near Coney Island. At the height of at least a thousand feet in the air a strange object was in the act of flying toward the New Jersey coast. It was apparently a man with bat's wings and improved frog's legs. The face of the man could be distinctly seen and it wore a cruel and determined expression. The movements made by the object closely resembled those of a frog in the act of swimming with his hind legs and flying with his front legs. When we add that this monster waved his wings in answer to the whistle of a locomotive and was of a deep black color, the alarming nature of the apparition can be imagined. The object was seen by many reputable persons and they all agree that it was a man engaged in flying toward New Jersey.

The article goes on to speculate that the flying anomaly could not possibly be an "aeronaut" due to the fact that such an inventor would surely be seeking publicity and financial gain for his feat. Instead, the article's author proposes a more diabolical and covert purpose behind the being's remarkable appearance. Further pertinent information is then offered: "About a month ago an object of precisely the same nature was seen in the air over St. Louis by a number of citizens who happened to be sober and are believed to be trustworthy. A little later it was seen by various Kentucky persons as it flew across the state. In no instance has it been known to alight, and no one has seen it at a lower elevation than a thousand feet above the surface of the Earth. It is without a doubt the most extraordinary and wonderful object that has ever been seen."

At this juncture, we certainly must not overlook the fact that newspapers of that particular era were prone to fabricating fabulous tales intended to increase circulation, as evidenced by the Great Moon Hoax from the same century.

The Van Meter Creature

If we are to put any stock at all in newspaper clippings of the time, then the town of Van Meter, Iowa, was under siege by a terrifying winged creature in October of 1903. A segment that appeared in New York's *Watertown Herald* told the story. The first victim was a doctor by the name of A. C. Olcott, who was taking a nap in his office on Principle Street one evening. The good doctor was abruptly disturbed from his slumber by a luminous flash. Startled, Olcott seized his shotgun and dashed out into the street in order to investigate. It was then that perhaps his greatest nightmare came to fruition as he was confronted by a humanoid monstrosity that was descending from the sky. The entity was possessing of massive, membranous wings and by all accounts displayed a beak, as well as a glowing horn on its head that emitted blinding light. Without hesitation, Dr. Olcott fired at the creature, causing it to pounce before taking to the air once again. Olcott detected a nauseating stench that the beast had left in its wake.

But the monster's rampage was far from over, since an armed guard at the local credit union evidently discharged his weapon at the apparition later that same evening. Additionally, still another doctor across town bore witness to the creature climbing a telephone pole and took action similar to his colleague by firing a shotgun in its general direction. Van Meter resident Sidney Gregg arrived just in time to watch the mutation bound away like a kangaroo.

By the following morning, the entire community of Van Meter was in a mini state of panic as they learned about the bone-chilling events that had transpired the night before. Validation was provided by a series of three-toed tracks that were discovered where the monster had been seen.

At twilight, as restless citizens prepared for a return visit, the foreman of the local brick factory discerned a troubling noise emanating from an abandoned mine shaft on the premises. As a crowd gathered, the ghastly creature emerged from its opening and was accompanied by a smaller companion, no less. Despite the monster's apparent invulnerability to firearms, multiple shots were fired, with evidently no result.

The final chapter of this epic describes the Van Meter Creature reentering the mine shaft entrance the following morning, thankfully never to be seen again.

Valkyrie of Voltana

In contrast to the majority of flying humanoid cases, the Spanish Voltana (Boltaña) episode appears to involve an apparition of the angelic variety. Voltana is a tiny village nestled in Spain's remote and scenic Pyrenees Mountains. In June 1905 the location was seemingly the epicenter for a miraculous series of events. I present the following excerpts from an article that was published in the *Indianapolis Sunday Star* on November 25 of that year:

Five times since the first day of June a woman, robed in white, with long clinging draperies, has flown over the town of Voltana in northern Spain, and the people of that entire district of the Pyrenees are in a state of religious fervor and excitement, expecting each day to hear the blast of a bugle...or the call of a voice from the skies. The astounding message of the fifth flight of the woman over the town has just been received at Barbasto, together with the state that scores of persons standing on the mountainside, scores in the streets of the town, and men from their homes and their fields knelt where they were and watched the flight.

The woman...or whatever it is...came from the northward each time...from the direction of gigantic Mt. Perdu...one of the highest peaks of the Pyrenees...and disappeared to the southwestward among the peaks of the Sierra de Guara. There was no sign of any balloon or wings or other appliances...It was as if a woman garbed as an angel but without wings floated over the town, slowly, unhurriedly...and three of the five times against a strong wind, blowing either from the south or the southwest.

The incidents were apparently investigated by a British mining expert on the scene, who confirmed that over 240 persons had witnessed the "mystic figure." And at least one villager claimed that she had heard a sound like joyful singing when the woman in white had flown overhead. But the unnerving visitation had a profound impact on some. For example, a mule driver named Pedro Pobrado "rushed into the church frightened almost out of his senses, and threw himself before the priest praying and imploring him to give absolution, declaring that the end of the world was coming and that the warning angel was flying through the sky."

As we can see, there are no variations of flying humanoids that are perceived as being purely benign.

Arsenyev's Flying Man

Vladimir Klavdiyevich Arsenyev was born in Petersburg, Russia, in 1872. As a young man, Vladimir dreamt of far wanderings in exotic and remote places. It was most assuredly this sense of adventure that landed him in military service at a young age. Eager to travel and explore, at the age of twenty-eight he petitioned for an assignment in the Russian Far East and was granted the rank of lieutenant, in addition to being placed in charge of a hunting command in Vladivostok. It was while stationed there that he gained his far-reaching reputation as an outstanding researcher, topographer, and naturalist. During 1906, Vladimir began to lead scientific expeditions into the mountainous Sikhote-Alin region at the behest of the Russian Geographical Society. His mission was to map and document the unexplored, temperate wilderness to the best of his ability. These explorations resulted in Vladimir writing a trilogy of extremely popular books. It was in his final edition, published posthumously in 1937, that his inexplicable encounter with a flying, manlike being was revealed.

One day, as Vladimir was hiking along an isolated trail with his dog in tow, he came upon an impression that greatly reminded him of a human footprint. As he was examining the spoor, his faithful companion began to growl and behave strangely, as if something was amiss. Without warning, they both detected the sound of a large animal moving through the brush and then coming to a sudden stop. Because the humid air was dense and foggy, Vladimir was unable to make out precisely what manner of strange beast stood before them. In an effort to bring clarity to the situation, he knelt down and picked up a rock, hurling it in the direction where the ominous presence was lurking. He couldn't possibly have anticipated what occurred next: "Then something happened that was quite unexpected. I heard the beating of wings. Something large and dark emerged from the fog and flew over the river. A moment later it disappeared into the dense mist. My dog, badly frightened, pressed itself to my feet." According to his account, the creature emitted a waning shriek or howl as it departed.

Vladimir was mystified by his odd encounter and mentioned it to his dinner hosts that same evening. "After supper I told the Udehe men about this incident. They broke into a vivid story about a man who could fly in the air. Hunters often saw his tracks, tracks that appeared suddenly and vanished suddenly, in such a way that they could only be possible if the 'man' alighted on the ground, then took off again into the air." Considering what an astute and experienced observer Vladimir Arsenyev was, we can hardly hope for a more credible source from which to draw our evidence.

This evidence may be reinforced by an article that appeared in a 1992 issue of *Fate Magazine*. According to Russian UFO experts Alexander Rempel and Paul Stonehill, there was a spate of winged-creature reports coming out of eastern Russia during 1991. One sighting involved a hunter named Kurentsov, who was camping very near the location where Vladimir had had his encounter almost a century earlier. According to Kurentsov, he had been awakened by the sound of a large, black creature descending close to his campfire. He was able to see that the thing possessed a human shape and webbed bat's wings. Fortunately, the man was unmolested.

Another encounter centered around the Ivanitzky family of Petropavlovsk, who found an utterly weird animal hiding under their bed one night. Following a chaotic fray, during which the family pelted the creature with slippers and poisoned it with household chemicals, the father disposed of its remains in a ditch. His greatest concern had been that it was some type of exotic or endangered species ,and he did not want to face any consequences for offing it. The Ivanitzkys described the thing as having five-foot leathery wings, three-fingered claws, blue fur, and a flat, primatelike face with large eyes and a lipless mouth. Perhaps the weirdest feature, however, was its triangular nose, which was capable of transforming into a trunklike appendage. At long last, Vladimir's flying man had been seen again…and it had a new name—Letay-uschiy Chelovek!

Angels of Mons

During the First World War, a modern myth was born. To this day, scholars declare that the entire affair was merely a huge misunderstanding or hoax, conceived out of religious zeal and a fictional story that was construed as being the gospel truth by many who read it.

The date was August 23, 1914, and British Expeditionary Forces were making a hard push toward the German front-lines in mainland Europe. Some 70,000 German troops had been deployed at the industrial city of Mons, Belgium, in an attempt to hold the left flank of a definitive Allied attack. However, the Allied commanders had greatly underestimated the strength of the opposition, and subsequently, the British found themselves outnumbered by a ratio of three to one.

The Brits fought valiantly that day and miraculously held their own, but the German forces prevailed, forcing them to eventually retreat. So courageous was the Allied effort that a legend was born. It is believed by some that a regiment of angels had interceded on behalf of the British that day.

The origin can probably be traced to gothic horror writer Arthur Machen. Shortly after the engagement at Mons, Machen had published a short story called "The Bowmen" in which he recounted a tale about British troops being rallied by a brigade of phantom archers led by St. George. Believing the account to be accurate, parish magazines of the era began to reprint the article, and many readers were so inspired by the telling that they accepted it tooth and nail. At one point, Machem attempted to clarify the story's fictional nature, but some simply would not have it. The premise evolved over time, and the ghostly archers were transformed into silvery angels who sailed about in the sky above the Mons battlefield, shooting fiery arrows at the Germans and protecting the lives of the British troops. This motif became so ingrained in the public consciousness that even some veterans of the battle were convinced they had actually seen the angels.

If nothing else, the story of the Angels of Mons stands as a reminder that the lines between fact and folklore are often blurred by people's perceptions.

Angel of Cabeco

On October 13, 1917, an event known as the Miracle of the Sun occurred at Fátima, Portugal. Between 70,000 and 100,000 people are said to have gathered in order to bear witness to a spectacular, divine revelation. Their wish was fulfilled when the clouds apparently parted, revealing a sun, which danced and changed colors before their very eyes. At one point, it even seemed as if the great star would crash into the Earth. The incident is well documented. But one of the central characters, a young nun named Lúcia Santos, claimed to have had prior visitations from spirits, including the Virgin Mary herself and even angels.

Lúcia's first encounter with the supernatural had taken place two years earlier, when she was overseeing a flock of sheep along with a trio of other girls—Teresa Maitias, Teresa's sister Maria, and little Maria Justino. The little shepherds were at Cabeco, a grassy, hilly area near the coast. As they glanced up into the sky, an apparition began to appear. "We'd had our lunch and were just beginning the Rosary when suddenly we saw, above the trees in the valley below us, a kind of cloud that was whiter than the snow. It was transparent and in human form," Lúcia recalled years later. The figure appeared amorphous and headless, and after a while it faded away and vanished from their sight. One girl was so shaken by the experience that she ran home to tell her mother about it. Following other self-professed miracles, Lúcia Santos concluded that the presence had, in fact, been that of an angel.

Magnificent Flying Creature of Hubbell, Nebraska

If we are to believe a dubious and vague fourth-hand account that has made the rounds in UFO circles for years, the great French ufologist Jacques Vallée discovered a fanciful account that had been hidden in a U.S. military dossier. It contained a correspondence from a man named William C. Lamb, who claimed that he was hunting near Hubbell, Nebraska, early in the morning of February 22, 1922, when the still silence was broken by an ultrasonic noise. Looking up, Lamb spotted a massive, shadowy form gliding through the air. It darkened the sky. Taking refuge in the woods, the hunter could see something descending, and, to his amazement, it appeared to be a "magnificent flying creature" that stood close to eight feet tall. The creature dashed by the astounded man, leaving its mark on the snowy ground. Lamb claimed that he attempted to track the being but that he wasn't able to catch up to it. In recent years, UFO researcher Chris Aubeck has uncovered evidence that William C. Lamb had been responsible for logging other questionable reports with officials, including claims of religious visions and conversations with God.

Manlike Figure
over Kazakhstan

While the dawn of the twentieth century played host to a mélange of flying humanoids ranging from apparent angels to bat-winged gargoyles, our perception of this paradigm was about to shift dramatically over the coming decades. The first hint came in 1936 when a fifteen-year-old girl in Pavlodar, Kazakhstan, had an unnerving rendezvous with an aerial, manlike object of an entirely new variety.

E. E. Loznaya was strolling to school one winter morning on an isolated path when she noticed an unusual object flying through the air. Within moments, the student was able to discern that the subject appeared to be a medium-sized man dressed in black overalls and donning a matching helmet that obscured its face. The figure was wearing an oval "rucksack" on its back and seemed to be emitting a low, rumbling noise. Imagine the young woman's terror when she realized that the being had changed directions and seemed to be headed straight toward her! Panicked, the fear-stricken girl tried to hide, but she found herself in the midst of a vast snowbank with nowhere to run to. When she glanced up again, the flying man had vanished.

TWO

Flying Saucer Invaders!

While the previous chapter highlighted some of the whimsical flying humanoid accounts that were gracing the pages of newspapers during the nineteenth and early twentieth centuries, this section focuses on reports from the mid- to latter-twentieth century, many of which seem to be linked to the UFO phenomenon that was quickly gaining notoriety around the globe. Like their predecessors, these airborne beings appeared to take on a variety of forms.

A New Age

World War II served as a backdrop for some of the most monumental atrocities in the history of mankind. This we must never forget. The conflict also resulted in rapid developments in technology, including aerial advancements. Da Vinci's helicopter had at last come to fruition by the late 1930s, and airplanes had evolved into single-bodied units with metal fuselages. Some of these possessed turbo jets that could achieve speeds close to 400 miles per hour.

The Germans had designed the first long-range rockets, including the infamous V2, which struck terror into the hearts of western Europe. But the biggest game changer was the introduction of the atom bomb, the most destructive weapon ever conceived. Delivered by high-flying B-29 bombers, its controversial use on the Japanese cities of Hiroshima and Nagasaki in August 1945 resulted in utter devastation and immense loss of life. Taking all of this into account, it's easy to understand how events of the time had a profound impact on humanity and our perception of mankind's seemingly newfound domination of the skies.

Shortly after the war had ended, on June 24, 1947, a businessman and aviator named Kenneth Arnold was flying his two-passenger plane near Mount Rainier, Washington, when he had a most remarkable encounter. Arnold had noticed a flash of light in the distance and subsequently observed nine silvery objects flying in formation that he couldn't identify. As he tracked them for several minutes, Arnold was completely baffled. The apparent crafts were traveling at incomprehensible speeds and did not produce a contrail. In addition, they seemed to have a convex shape and were lacking wings.

Upon landing, he reported the strange sighting to officials. But it was his statement to the press that had a resonating effect. Arnold had colored the objects' movements as resembling "saucers skipping across the water."

For better or worse, the term "flying saucer" had entered the public psyche, and it wasn't long before notions of extraterrestrial origin were suggested. For the first time, humans were seriously contemplating the possibility that we are not alone.

Aeronauts over Washington State

Chehalis, Washington, lies within a stone's throw of Mount Rainier, where Kenneth Arnold's sighting had ushered in a new age of aerial mysteries. Less than a year after the Arnold incident, on January 6, 1948, Bernice Zaikowski of Chehalis observed a man flying through the air just after 3:00 p.m. According to newspaper articles from the time, Mrs. Zaikowski, a sixty-one-year-old Polish immigrant, had first spotted the being gliding in from the northwest after detecting a "whizzing" sound. By the time the figure was over her farm, she was able to estimate that the man appeared to be about 200 feet up in the air and possessed enormous, metallic wings that were strapped to his body. The wings never flapped or rotated at any point. On the aeronaut's breast was some sort of control panel that he was using to guide his movements. Eventually, the entity ascended at a rapid speed as his airfoils retracted close to his body.

In the interim, several neighborhood children had gathered on the Zaikowski property in order to watch in awe as the being flew away to the south. Despite this fact, authorities including local law enforcement as well as the military did not put much stock in the report.

But just three months later on April 9, a pair of laundry workers forty miles to the south of Chehalis experienced something strikingly similar. Viola Johnson of Longview, Washington, had just stepped outside for a breath of fresh air when she noticed three objects in the sky that she at first took to be big birds. As the creatures drew nearer, it became obvious to her that they were humanoid in form. Viola later explained, "They wore dark, drab flying suits and as far as I can judge... I'm not very good at judging distance... they were about two hundred and fifty feet high, circling the city. They were going about the same speed as a freight train, and had some kind of apparatus at their sides, which looked like guns, but I know it couldn't have been guns. I couldn't see any propellers or any motors tied on them, but I could hear motors, which sounded about like airplane motors... only not so loud." Co-worker James Pittman was alerted to the situation by a panic-stricken Viola and made it outside just in time to see the figures disappear out of sight.

The absurdity of the situation is put into perspective when we consider some of Viola's other observations: "I couldn't make out their arms but I could see their legs dangling down and they kept moving their heads like they were looking around. I couldn't tell if they had goggles on, but their heads looked like they had helmets on. I couldn't see their faces." One local newspaper characterized the beings as "motorized birdmen."

Obviously, we must take into account the fact that the first jet packs were not successfully flown until 1959, ruling out the likelihood that these events were related to military testing. Some researchers have suggested that Zaikowski's winged Chehalis flyer was simply a man hang gliding. But the fact that his legs were dangling vertically refute this theory, since hang gliders must keep their bodies horizontal at all times.

Flatwoods Monster

It soon came to pass that in the years following Kenneth Arnold's sighting, a wave of so-called flying saucer (also known as UFO) reports began to surface all over the United States. One of the most exceptional incidents centered around a creature that became known as the Flatwoods Monster—also referred to as the Braxton County Monster, as well as the Green Monster. Though not a flying humanoid in the tradition of our batmen and winged angels, the subject did appear to be generally humanoid in shape, according to eyewitnesses, and it did hover or float above the ground exclusively while in view. For years, writers have sensationalized certain aspects of the case, but the consistent details as conveyed by those who saw it are apparently not lacking in any way.

Flatwoods is a tiny, rural community in mountainous Braxton County, West Virginia. It's the kind of place where everyone knows everyone else and where salt-of-the-earth, blue-collar families go about their business with little fanfare. Just before dusk on the evening of September 12, 1952, a group of local boys were playing football in the town's school-yard when one of them shouted something to the effect of, "What on earth is that?" The others looked up just in time to see a massive flaming object soaring through the sky. The boys all described the thing as being about the size of a house and having an oval or spheroid shape. Its color was bright or-ange and red. As they watched it, the object slowed down and descended on the top of the highest peak at the northern edge of town. Perhaps drawing off of each other's brazen courage and enthusiasm, the mob decided that the thing must be a meteor, or perhaps even one of the flying saucers that they had been reading about in the papers. Either way, they were determined to find out precisely what it was.

The mob ran toward the direction where they had seen the thing land, making a pit stop at the house of one of the boys, where adults Kathleen May and Eugene Lemon joined the posse.

Kathleen was a beautician in her twenties who had just gotten home from work. She was exhausted but didn't want the children climbing unsupervised the steep, wooded hill in the dark. Eugene was eighteen years old and had recently enlisted in the army. He brought his trusty dog along on the trek. Kathleen and Eugene led the way, brandishing flashlights, with five boys ranging in age from eight to fourteen trailing behind.

As the group ascended a pathway to the farm where they believed the object to be, some noticed a glowing, pulsing light through the trees on their right-hand side. An unpleasant, stannic odor was present in the air. As they neared the top of the incline, the group could hear a sizzling-popping sound and suddenly spotted two red eyes peering at them from a height of about twelve feet off the ground. Kathleen swung the beam of her flashlight upward toward the object in question. At that moment, an immense figure lit up like a Christmas tree and came to life.

Whatever the thing was, all who were present were in agreement that it generally displayed a humanlike form, though it was towering at least nine feet above them. Furthermore, the monster was hovering in the air at least a foot off the ground. Intense beams of light shot out of its eyes as it began to move across the trail in front of them, scanning the surrounding area as it went. Eugene lost his legs and fell to the ground, inhaling a dose of an oily fluid that had filled the air. His dog had long since retreated with its tail between its legs and had taken off back down the hill. The others quickly followed suit and began to run pell-mell for safety. No words were uttered as they all fled down the path, at one point hurdling a high fence like Olympic athletes.

When the frazzled group finally reached the May residence, several of the boys began vomiting, perhaps a combination of fear and the overpowering fumes they had all inhaled. Eugene's dog had already vomited on the veranda and would mysteriously die within days of the incident.

Kathleen May phoned the local police. As fate would have it, at the time, most of the law enforcement officials in the area were miles to the south investigating a report of an "airplane" crash. Undoubtedly the two events were related somehow. But one deputy did show up within the hour to investigate the incident, along with a local reporter. It was obvious to both of them that all of the witnesses were still scared out of their wits and that several of them were feeling deathly ill. When the deputy and reporter eventually located the spot where the monster had been seen, whatever it was that the group had encountered was nowhere to be found, nor was there any sign of the UFO that had been spotted by the boys. The investigators did detect a metallic smell lingering in the area and some type of oily substance on the ground.

Journalist A. Lee Stewart interviewed Kathleen May, Eugene Lemon, and the five boys who were present and had them individually sketch the creature they had seen. The drawings were virtually identical. All present had estimated that the monster had been at least nine or ten feet tall and that its head was shaped like the ace of spades, with a round face and two eyes that resembled portholes.

No other facial features were discernible. The being did not appear to have limbs, just antennae sticking out where the arms should have been, and its body looked like an upside-down ice cream cone with pleats or hoses running vertically down its side. Its entire mass had seemed to be internally illuminated. That aspect, along with the fact that it had sputtered a smelly, oily liquid and had made mechanical noises, seemed to indicate that the "monster" had in fact been some type of machine. It has been postulated that what was observed may have been some type of spacesuit, perhaps piloted by a living creature within it.

This theory has been further reinforced by researcher and author Frank Feschino, who has written the definitive books on the case. Feschino managed to locate a family who apparently encountered the monster the night after the Flatwoods incident and only a few miles away from where it had been seen previously. On this occasion, the creature seemed to appear mechanical below the waist but was definitively flesh and blood above, indicating that perhaps it had discarded the upper section of its spacesuit at some point. The distraught family's car had broken down on a remote stretch of road, and soon after, the humanoid being had emerged from the surrounding forest and then placed its hand on the hood of their vehicle before departing.

Feschino also discovered that the military had dispatched a National Guard unit to Flatwoods the night of the initial sighting and had in fact focused on the case as part of its comprehensive UFO investigation called Project Blue Book. It is also interesting that Flatwoods lies a mere one hundred miles east of the township of Point Pleasant, West Virginia, which was the site of the extensive Mothman saga that we will address in a subsequent chapter.

Houston Batman

Anyone who has ever spent a summer in Houston, Texas, knows how truly oppressive the intense heat and humidity can be. It is expressly for this reason that Hilda Walker was sitting out on the front porch of her apartment building on the evening of June 18, 1953. Hilda, a twenty-three-year-old housewife, was lounging and chatting with her neighbors, fourteen-year-old Judy Meyers and thirty-three-year-old Howard Phillips, a tool plant inspector.

Back in those days, air-conditioning units weren't nearly as common as they are today, which resulted in many restless nights in the South. The apartment building was located at 118 East Third Street in Houston's historic Heights neighborhood, just northwest of downtown.

Suddenly, Hilda noticed a huge shadow crossing the lawn. At first she assumed the shadow had been caused by a large moth fluttering in front of the nearby streetlight, but then the trio watched the thing shoot up onto the branch of a huge pecan tree. It was then that they realized it was something quite unknown.

As their eyes adjusted, all three witnesses could make out the form of a tall man standing almost seven feet high. He possessed batlike wings. While they sat there "stupefied," other details emerged. The being seemed to be adorned in a dark, tight-fitting uniform of some sort. Though the most miraculous aspect was the fact that the imposing apparition appeared to be surrounded by a radiant glow of light. For about thirty seconds (although it must have felt like much longer to the stunned witnesses), the figure rocked back and forth on a thick branch. That's when the light slowly began to fade and the Batman completely vanished from view. At that moment, Judy cried out in terror.

A short time later, there was a loud sound like wind rushing on the other side of the street, and they all watched a blinding, rocket-shaped flash of light shoot up into the air at incredible speed. Hilda was so unnerved by the experience that she contacted the police the very next day.

When later interviewed by a reporter for the *Houston Chronicle*, Judy Meyers stated, "I saw it and nobody can say I didn't." Howard Phillips added, "I've heard so much about flying saucer stories and I thought all those people telling the stories were crazy, but now I don't know what to believe . . . I saw it, whatever it was."

As a longtime resident of Houston, I can contribute a couple of personal anecdotes to this case. First, the location where the incident took place is no longer in existence. It has since been cleared away to make room for a stretch of

Interstate 10. Also, I once heard a secondhand story about a goliath of a man who was seen crouching down on the roof of a downtown building. The observers were employees of Houston's famous Bellaire Theater. It appeared to them as if the entity were wearing some kind of helmet and was attempting to hide, despite his massive girth. I like to think that perhaps they spotted the Batman. Maybe, just maybe...he's still lurking in my old hometown.

Under Siege by Floating Goblins

It seems fitting to include the much-documented Kelly/Hopkinsville, Kentucky, UFO incident that allegedly involved encounters with unearthly, little beings that have been generally referred to as goblins. Of relevance here is the reputed ability of these entities to float in the air, seemingly impervious to gravity.

The events of August 15, 1955, if true, are reminiscent of the flying saucer invasion films that were popular at the time. It is a story so unbelievable that we would be quick to dismiss it if not for the fact that the creatures were seen by several reputable people on that fateful night and that local officials were impressed enough by their emotional state to call over a dozen officers immediately to the scene in order to investigate. Indeed, the witnesses were so traumatized by the affair that the entire family moved out of their residence shortly thereafter, never to return.

The conflict occurred at the farmhouse of the Sutton family in a very rural hamlet called Kelly, which lies just eight miles north of the town of Hopkinsville, Kentucky. Billy Ray Taylor and his young wife were visiting from Pennsylvania at the time, and Billy Ray had stepped outside around 7:00 p.m. in order to retrieve some water from the well. A few minutes later he returned visibly distraught, insisting that he had seen an illuminated, disc-shaped object seemingly land in a gully several hundred yards away. Thinking at first that he was pulling their legs, or perhaps had seen a shooting star, the Sutton family disregarded his claim. A short while later, though, their dog began to bark uncontrollably and sought refuge under the porch. Patriarch Elmer "Lucky" Sutton and Billy Ray did what any God-fearing Southerners would do when confronted by a sketchy situation: they grabbed a shotgun and headed outside to deal with it.

But the two men literally stopped dead in their tracks when they were confronted by a three-foot-tall, silvery humanoid that was rapidly approaching them with its hands held straight up in the air. Interpreting it to be an act of aggression rather than surrender, Elmer fired on the monstrosity, which apparently had no effect, since the apparition merely did a backflip and vanished from sight. The men immediately retreated to the safety of the house where the same, or perhaps a second, goblin was seen peeking through the window, resulting in Elmer's teenage son, J. C. Sutton, firing off a shotgun blast that punctured the glass. Strangely, the Peeping Tom was left apparently unscathed once again.

When Lucky Sutton (an ironic name, considering the situation) and Billy Ray crept outside to surmise the damage, a clawed hand dropped down from the awning and grabbed Billy Ray by his hair in true horror-film fashion. The men opened fire on this goblin, which was crawling around on the roof, as well as at an identical creature that was seen perched on a high tree branch. The bullets apparently all hit their marks, but the intruders were consistently unharmed and even floated slowly to the ground instead of falling.

The remainder of the evening was spent engaged in a mini war of the worlds, with the entire property being riddled by a barrage of bullets that were being fired by the Sutton clan at the unwelcome invaders. Though three young children remained huddled in terror under a bed during the ordeal, all of the adults got a good look at the creatures.

Everyone present was in agreement that the bizarre beings had muscular torsos and long arms, but that their legs appeared to be withered and weak. The beings walked with an awkward, pivoting motion, and their most prevalent features were large, pointy ears and bulging, yellow eyes on the sides of their heads. They had no visible noses and only a slit where their mouths should have been. Their large hands resembled webbed talons. Whenever the creatures were struck by ammunition, the resulting impacts produced metallic plunking sounds. After a few hours, the besieged family had finally had enough and piled into two vehicles, escaping into Hopkins-ville, where they drove directly to the sheriff's office.

The sheriff was apparently impressed by the utter panic and fear in their trembling voices as the group recounted their unbelievable tale. It seemed to him that they were all completely sober and consistent in their details, and he had never known the Sutton family to be afraid of anything be-fore. Ultimately, the encounter made newspaper headlines the next day and was even investigated by the military.

Several explanations have been put forward to explain the Kelly/Hopkinsville incident, including escaped mon-keys covered in silver paint (perhaps a theory more ridicu-lous than the notion of invading aliens), or a misidentifi-cation of some aggressive owls that were merely defending their territory, resulting in ensuing hysteria.

These suggestions just don't carry much weight when we consider the number of witnesses present and the fact that their stories have always remained unwavering. To this day, the few survivors of the siege have stuck to their convictions that something truly extraordinary occurred at the Sutton farm that evening. This is born out by the fact that other resi-dents, including a responding police officer, reported seeing strange lights in the sky over Kelly that night.

Nebraska's
Demonic Winged Entity

As our next account would suggest, rural farming communities were becoming somewhat of a mecca for all manner of flying humanoids by the mid-1950s. One eyewitness, who no doubt feared potential ridicule, filed a report that was published under the pseudonym John Hanks.

According to "Mr. Hanks" of Falls City, Nebraska, he was confronted by a nine-foot-tall nonhuman entity in 1956. His startling description of the creature sounds reminiscent of something out of an H. P. Lovecraft story. Hanks stated the being had two shiny, fifteen-foot-long aluminum-looking wings strapped to its body that appeared to have multicolored lights running along their underside and that the humanoid was evidently manipulating a control panel attached to his chest. Most disturbing was the creature's demonic face, which featured large, watery, blue eyes and skin that resembled wrinkled leather. The thing emitted a hissing sound as it flew overhead about fifteen feet off the ground. Hanks was understandably paralyzed with fear as the monster passed overhead.

We must acknowledge similarities to the Chehalis, Washington, incident discussed at the start of this chapter. In particular the silver metallic wings attached by straps, in addition to a chest-mounted control panel.

Unidentified Flying Things in the United Kingdom

While many unsettling encounters lay ahead in the decades following the 1960s, a precursor of things to come took place at Sandling Park in Hythe, Kent, England, on November 16, 1963. The southern British Isles would eventually be the stage for the macabre Owlman saga that would occur almost thirteen years later. But on that particular cold evening, four young people claimed they saw something incomprehensible that stalked them for several minutes.

Seventeen-year-old John Flaxton and eighteen-year-old Mervyn Hutchinson, along with two of their mates, were out for a nighttime walk on a quiet country lane when John observed a luminous object, similar to a bright star, hovering in the stratosphere above them. The quartet quickly realized that something was amiss when the light descended from the sky in an unprecedented manner and began to pursue them relentlessly. The youths collectively felt an ominous chill as the object followed along behind them. It had an oval shape, was golden in color, and stayed about two hundred feet behind the nervous observers as it floated about ten feet off the ground. At one point, the boys temporarily lost sight of the orb behind some trees, right around the time that a horrifying, dark-colored apparition emerged from the woods where they had last seen it vanish.

Before fleeing in terror, John, along with the others, saw that the creature was man-sized, though it also had substantial batlike wings and webbed feet similar to a duck's. Oddly, the thing seemed to be completely lacking a head. The fearsome phantom began to shuffle toward them as if intending harm, though the boys didn't stick around long enough to find out what its intentions were.

Authorities and UFO investigators were duly impressed with the testimony of the four lads who had mustered up the courage to return with them to the location the next day. It was then that nine-inch impressions resembling tracks were found stamped in the ground.

Manlike Figure Flies over Pine Land Plantation

Reports from the southeastern United States are somewhat fleeting, but something resembling a man was apparently seen floating over the state of Mississippi on September 1, 1966. The primary witness was Mrs. James Ikart, who first noticed the anomaly at around 2:00 p.m. hovering over Pine Land Plantation. For a considerable amount of time, Mrs. Ikart observed the figure fall to lower altitudes before ascending up into the heavens. She couldn't make out much in the way of details but thought that the being appeared to be white in color. Local officials speculated that the object may have been a weather balloon, though other residents from the town of Scott evidently watched the thing as well.

The year 1966 turned out to be the banner year for the flying humanoid phenomenon, as we will discover in a subsequent chapter.

More Little Men From...

The file cabinets of UFO researchers are jammed with reports of nonhuman entities in a variety of forms. These beings are typically observed in the company of their presumed craft, which also demonstrate many delineations, though the flying saucer types seem most prevalent. One such account was published in a French newspaper years ago. It involves two children who are only listed by the names of François and Anne-Marie.

On the morning of August 29, 1967, the youths were tending to a herd of cattle near the tiny village of Cussac when they noticed a brilliant, spherical object resting upon legs that resembled landing gear. The globule was some 200 feet away and partially obscured by brush, but the children could evidently see four diminutive humanoid figures with black skin or tight-fitting garments standing close by it.

The little beings appeared to have large heads with prominent chins and long, spindly arms. Their faces featured pointy noses and beards, and their legs were stubby with webbed feet. As François and Anne-Marie watched for about thirty seconds, the entities floated into the air and were quite literally absorbed by the ball of light. Moments later, the sphere shot up into the air and out of sight.

Policemen and other officials who investigated the scene noticed a smell like sulfur and discovered a scorched patch on the ground. The children claimed that their cows were acting strangely during the incident, and François apparently had a noticeable irritation in his eyes that lasted for days.

Another European encounter took place just before midnight on December 7, 1978. An Italian man named Alfonso Marinelli was driving near the community of Navelli when his car engine suddenly stalled. As Alfonso exited his vehicle, he spotted two mysterious lights approaching him from the air about forty feet off the ground. When they drew closer, Marinelli saw that the objects were in fact little men dressed in shiny uniforms with flattened, oblong helmets and lights strapped to their chests. The creatures were flying along in an upright position and didn't make a sound as they passed by him, eventually turning around before heading back the way they came. Once the figures had disappeared from sight, Marinelli was able to start his car again and continue his journey.

In his book *Curious Encounters*, author Loren Coleman opens with the strange saga of Robert and Jackie Bair, a truck-driving couple who allegedly entered a restaurant in Sauk Centre, Minnesota, on October 8, 1984, in a state of near panic. The Bairs informed anyone who would listen that they had been accosted by small birdlike creatures with pointy heads and human feet. According to the couple, the airborne gremlins had been pursuing them and firing shards of metal at their truck for several hours, ever since they had witnessed a "spaceship" crash near Billings, Montana. A local reporter who interviewed the Bairs at length found them both to be sincere in their belief that they had experienced something far beyond their understanding.

———————

To what do we owe these disconcerting tales? One would certainly be justified in dismissing these stories as deliberate concoctions or perhaps the product of advanced dementia. However, the evidence is still mounting that we share our planet with baffling visitors that glide about in the air with reckless abandon.

Nearly two decades after Kenneth Arnold first glimpsed his flying saucers over Mount Rainier, Washington, there had been no reprieve. In fact, all indications point to the contrary. Encounters with all manner and types of mind-boggling intruders had continued and even proliferated at an alarming rate.

Still, the most notable episode of all was about to unfold in an unassuming community on the banks of the Ohio River. Over the course of a year, dozens—or perhaps even hundreds—of seemingly normal people would bear witness to a winged monster that continues to mystify us. Mothman … the king off all flying humanoids was about to make his grand entrance.

THREE

The Manbirds

In this chapter, we will address modern accounts of humanoids that appear to display wings, feathers, and other characteristics of birds. From a purely scientific point of view, this concept is very hard to swallow, no pun intended. Evolution just simply does not work this way, and in fact, genetically speaking, humans and other primates are so far removed from the class of Aves that it is truly a biological impossibility. Curiously though, mythologies around the world do tell of such creatures, with the Harpies of Ancient Greece serving as perhaps the most well-known example. Yet, during the latter part of the twentieth century, anthropomorphic birdmen from the pages of mythology were allegedly on the prowl once again. It almost seemed as though the old religion were holding a modern revival of sorts. In the following pages are some striking examples.

"Owlman Plate" © Thomas E. Finley

Brazilian Bird People

One of the greatest experiences of my life was traveling throughout the continent of South America when I was but a lad. My mother, who had been in remission from cancer at the time, had a newfound zeal for life and wanted to expose me and my sister to faraway lands and new experiences. Among the wonders that we were fortunate enough to see were the lofty and mysterious Inca ruins of Machu Picchu in the Andes Mountains, as well as the diverse natural wonders of the Galapagos Islands.

Still, I will never forget the adventure of camping along the mighty Amazon River, deep in the emerald jungle. Like all boys, I was careless in my fascination for living things and broke every rule, from handling a colorful but deadly poisonous caterpillar to splashing around in the piranha-infested waters.

We were introduced to the primitive Yagua and Javaro tribes, living in a perpetual state of harmony with nature and relatively unaffected by the encroaching influence of the twentieth century. I was profoundly struck by the remoteness, the vastness of this veritable lost world. Surely, if there is anywhere on the planet where strange, new creatures lurk, the Green Continent just might be the place.

Summarily, sometime during the 1950s, two exceedingly strange creatures were apparently encountered in southern Brazil near the coastal city of Pelotas. According to a South American journal that was published in 1976, Lucy Gerlach Réal and her husband Luiz de Rosario Réal were strolling down a forested path one evening when they observed a pair of swift, moonlit silhouettes gracing the trail ahead of them.

As the couple glanced up into the air, they discerned what they believed to be two enormous birds sailing over the tops of the trees. But by the time the animals landed just ahead of them, it was evident that the two figures were in fact taller than any bird... and eerily humanlike.

While Lucy and Luiz watched in amazement, the beings stooped down as if trying to remain hidden from sight. The unnerved couple had an uneasy feeling, as if they were now being stalked by the creatures. They swiftly departed the scene, although Luiz later confessed that he had wanted to stay behind in order to determine the identity of the beings. Perhaps we shall never know their true character.

A Modern–day Tengu

In the appendix at the end of this book, I highlight the Tengu, a folkloric man-bird that plays a prominent role in Japanese culture. Interestingly enough, in 1952 at Camp Okubo (near Kyoto, Japan) a U.S. Air Force private named Sinclair Taylor reported shooting at something that looked remarkably similar to one of these mythical beings. According to his testimonial, which appeared in a 1983 edition of *Fate Magazine*, Taylor was standing guard one evening when he detected a sound like wings flapping. Looking up, he spotted what he at first took to be an enormous bird hovering over him, as if to attack. Taylor got the sense that the animal was leering at him with evil intent.

As the "bird" got closer, he prepared to discharge his rifle at the imposing creature. That's when he got the fright of his life. He explains, "The thing, which now had started slowly to descend again, had the body of a man. It was well over seven feet from head to feet, and its wingspread was almost equal to its height. I started to fire and emptied my carbine where the thing hit the ground. But when I looked up to see if my bullets had found home there was nothing there."

Upon investigating the incident, Taylor's superior officer informed him that another guard had encountered the same entity a year prior.

Birdman of Madisonville

On April 5, 1956, a being resembling a winged angel was allegedly sighted by workers at a steel plant in Birmingham, Alabama. As it flew over them in a northerly direction flapping its wings, the employees could tell that the subject was silver in color. Perhaps this was the same apparition that continuously stalked the forests near the town of Madisonville, Tennessee, which lies a mere two hundred miles to the north of Birmingham. Volunteer State native and UFO researcher Brent Raynes interviewed Mark Boring, editor of the *Monroe County Buzz* newspaper, who uncovered the story. The innuendo dates back to the year 1964 or so, and the phantom was reputedly seen many times by local teenagers who frequented a wooded hangout known as Hiwassee Knobs. At first the creature was believed to be an enormous bird, since its freak-ishly large form was typically observed flying high up in the air. But Boring himself claimed to have seen the thing as a youth and felt that it was really something quite unknown.

Things took a turn for the strange when a group of Boring's schoolmates spotted the "bird" on the ground on one occasion and chased it. They had claimed that the beast, which stood at least six or seven feet tall, ran away from them like a man. Then, as local legends often do, the stories spread. The Birdman was sighted everywhere, including perched on top of the local water tower.

Some residents claimed to have taken photos of it, which could never be located, and others were said to have shot at the monster with both bullets and arrows. A local hunter even confided that he had blasted off part of the thing's foot, but the Smithsonian Institute had apparently taken the spec-imen away for testing.

Sightings of the Madisonville Birdman seem to have trailed off by the early 1970s. Perhaps the much-maligned apparition had finally had enough of his teenage tormen-tors and decided to migrate to another locale.

Angel of Ecuador

In his book *Supernatural Strangers*, prolific writer Robert Tra-lins recounts a romantic tale of a South American birdman with heroic qualities. He tells the tale:

High in the Andes Mountains about seventy-five kilometers from Quito is the town of El Angel, where Vera Olaechea, a fourteen-year-old school girl, and Emilio Espinoza, her fifteen-year-old classmate, reside. On the morning of October 15, 1966, Vera and Emilio were climbing over the rocks of a high peak searching for wild bird eggs in the hidden nests there. Suddenly Vera slipped and fell headlong over the precipice. Fortunately, she managed to grab at some shrubs, which were growing out of a narrow shelf-like ledge on the rocks; it kept her for that terrible moment from dropping to her death hundreds of feet to the jagged rocks below.

Emilio bravely climbed over the rocks and tried to reach her, but he had nothing to hold onto. He had to wrap his legs around a rock and dangle head downward in order to give her a hand. As he did so, the rocks to which he was clinging with his legs began to topple, threatening to fall over the cliff and carry him and Vera to their deaths. At that moment when all seemed lost, there was suddenly a great flapping sound like some giant bird near at hand. A huge figure descended in the air and then strong hands caught them both and lifted them to safety. Dazed, the two children looked around them and saw, flying away, a huge white man-bird. An instant later it vanished into the clouds.

The two astounded youths scrambled back to their village and told anyone who would listen about their miraculous rescue from certain death by an "angel," which Emilio described as having snowy white wings. Much to their wonder and surprise, Vera and Emilio were told that in years past, other children from the village had also been rescued by the mysterious being who was viewed as their protector. Hence the name of the town … El Angel.

Mexico's Massive Winged Beings

A Mexican newspaper published some intriguing photos in September 1967. The images were reputed to be of enormous footprints that had been left by a winged giant that was encountered by a night watchman off Route 57 near San Luis Potosi. The witness's name was José Padron, and he had been awoken at around 1:00 a.m. on August 30 when he heard a disturbance at a construction site that he was responsible for overseeing. José was accustomed to dealing with marauding predators, petty thieves, and unruly vandals, but nothing in his years of experience had prepared him for what he was about to face.

When José exited his diminutive tin guard shack in order to investigate a loud ruckus, he claimed that he was confronted by a large creature with wings the size of a small airplane. The towering figure was striding fast in his direction, which understandably was causing José a great degree of distress. What should he do? Confront something that was beyond his comprehension, or flee for safety?

José wisely chose discretion over valor and scrambled to the safety of his tiny shelter, bolting the door behind him and hiding in a corner until the following morning. Much to his relief, he was sure that he had heard the sound of great beating wings, as if whatever it was that he had seen had departed the area.

The following morning, chief engineer Enrique Rueda arrived on site and found poor José in a sorry state. At first, Rueda was skeptical about the watchman's story, until he discovered a set of large three-toed tracks adjacent to a barricade fence. The impressions were more than twelve inches wide and sunken half a foot deep into the earth! By Rueda's calculations, whatever had made them must have weighed several hundred pounds.

The winged monster evidently returned to the construction site that very same night, and this time it had a companion. José observed both entities from a distance, careful not to alert them to his presence. When the enormous creatures took off, the force of their launch caused the ground to quake, and the hefty branch of a tall mesquite tree was snapped off at its base.

A dozen guards who were assigned to patrol the location the following evening must have served as a deterrent, because there was not a third appearance there. Though some American tourists staying at the nearby Cactus Hotel claimed that they saw three huge animals flying overhead on the evening of September 1.

Extraordinary
Bird Woman of Da Nang

Military outposts do not seem to intimidate flying human-oids. In fact, it is quite the opposite. It appears as though these creatures are rather attracted to these installations for some unknown reason. In addition to Private Sinclair Taylor's encounter mentioned earlier in the chapter, there is the account of Spring-heeled Jack accosting a British soldier who was standing sentry at his post in 1877, as well as the foreboding Scottish Skree that flew over a battlefield in 1746. We must wonder, therefore, if there is a link between these beings and the bloody carnage associated with war. But let us digest all of the data first.

During the Vietnam conflict, perhaps the creepiest of all winged apparitions made an ominous appearance. The encounter was related to UFO researcher Don Worley by one of the U.S. Marines who encountered the abomination while on guard duty in the summer of 1969. PFC Earl Morrison was perched on top of a bunker with two other soldiers when their collective attention was drawn to something flying in their direction.

Morrison reflected, "We saw what looked like wings, like a bat's, only it was gigantic compared to what a regular bat would be. After it got close enough so we could see what it was. It looked like a woman. A naked woman. She was black. Her skin was black, the wings were black, everything was black. But it glowed. It glowed in the night... kind of a greenish cast to it."

One can scarcely imagine what went through the soldiers' minds as they tried to make sense of what they were observing. Morrison told Worley, "We watched her go straight over the top of us, and still she didn't make any noise flapping her wings. She blotted out the moon once...That's how close she was to us. And dark...looked like pitch black then, but we could still define her because she just glowed."

The three men watched the flying woman for several minutes as she drifted out of sight. They could eventually hear the sound of her wings flapping in the distance.

Morrison's description as told to Worley contained other startling facts. The winged woman had evidently possessed long, flowing hair on her head, and her entire body from top to bottom looked like it was covered with fur. In addition, the Bird Woman's hands seemed to be molded to her leathery wings, and both her arms and wings had "rippled" as if they were lacking the rigidity of bones.

I am reminded of a legendary Welsh witch known as the Gwrach-y-rhibyn, who is said to possess batlike wings and withered arms. But Vietnam and Wales are a world apart...or perhaps that's what the rational mind wants to believe.

Pajaro Hombre

In my book *Big Bird! Modern Sightings of Flying Monsters*, I chronicled decades of reports of enormous, unknown animals soaring over the low plains of southern Texas. The descriptions are divided, with some witnesses stating they observed charcoal-colored raptors resembling gargantuan buzzards, while many others insist that what they saw resembled poignantly prehistoric airborne reptiles known as pterodactyls. Throughout the course of my research, I came across a third type of winged Texan creature that was ostensibly manlike in nature.

Rumors of this man-bird first surfaced around Rio Grande City in Starr County, which lies on the Mexican border. Back in 1975, residents of that old, historic town began to speak of an apparition that was frequently seen lurking on the rooftops of the local tavern, as well as the county courthouse. The being was believed to be an abomination of bird and man, and his appearance predicated a rash of Big Bird reports that rocked the Rio Grande Valley in the early part of 1976.

A similar state of affairs exists in Robstown, which is located about 150 miles northeast of Starr County. I visited this small city in 2006 and was told about a *Pajaro Hombre* (Bird Man) that was familiar to residents there. Local barber and historian Joe Avalos was gracious enough to give me a tour of Robstown and led me to an abandoned cantina where the creature had often been a topic of discussion.

According to Avalos, the stories could be traced back to a homeless man who always wore black and who informed anyone who would listen that he could transform himself into a great bird when conditions were favorable. Avalos was of the opinion that the man had been a delusional drunkard and that his yarns were the result of his drunken binges, intended to solicit attention and perhaps the occasional handout or shot of tequila. Joe quipped to me, "That man drank so much that he was flying in his head." Sadly, the "bird man" of Robstown tragically died in a house fire, according to Avalos.

A dubious Texas case that gained media attention originated in the ironically named border community of Eagle Pass. A resident named Francisco Magallanes Jr. claimed that he had been attacked by a winged, manlike monster on his property late one evening in 1976. The twenty-one-year-old told police that he went into his backyard around 12:45 a.m. in order to investigate a loud noise and spotted a nightmarish creature in a stooped position. According to Magallanes, the bat-winged creature then rose to a height of six feet and pounced on him, scratching him badly in the ensuing struggle. Francisco somehow managed to break free from its grasp and ran inside his house to safety. Upon questioning by authorities, he revealed other details, describing the creature as having a pig's face with glowing red eyes and pointy ears; in addition to long arms, it had stubby legs and wings that extended eight feet. Magallanes also alleged that the all-black being had made a hissing sound like a snake and that while it was attacking him, his skin had felt like it was on fire. Apparently, a doctor who examined Francisco shortly after the incident concluded that his injuries were authentic. But it later turned out that the physician had been a close family friend. After further interrogation by the police, Magallanes admitted that he had been drinking heavily at the time, and soon inconsistencies in his story began to surface. As a result, most researchers now view this particular incident as a deliberate fabrication.

Owlman

If Mothman is the king of flying humanoids, then the only legitimate challenger to the throne is England's macabre Owlman, which has been encountered by nearly a dozen young people on various occasions beginning in 1976. Owlman's singular haunt is the forest surrounding Mawnan Church, a stone antiquity that rests on an ancient earthwork above the Helford River in Cornwall, adjacent to Falmouth Bay.

The area is famous for sightings of a sea serpent known as Morgawr, and it is for that reason that monster hunter Tony "Doc" Shiels was touring the region at the time. Shiels is an exceedingly colorful character and self-proclaimed wizard, who earns his living as an actor, magician, artist, writer, and all-around scallywag. During Easter weekend of the year in question, Doc and his unconventional family were performing a play at a local festival when he was approached by a distressed man named Don Melling, who accused Shiels of concocting an elaborate monster hoax that had frightened Melling's daughters.

The two girls, June (age 12) and Vicky (age 9), had been playing among the gravesites surrounding Mawnan Church when they noticed a weird sound and apparently observed a big, gray-feathered "bird man" hovering above the sanctuary's tower. So shaken were the girls that they ran screaming back to the picnic site where their parents were relaxing and alerted them. Don could tell that his children were utterly freaked out, so he quickly piled the family into their motorcar and sped away posthaste. Later that day, as the family was attempting to forget their ordeal, they ran into Shiels, and Mr. Melling confronted him about the incident. Although Shiels adamantly denied any involvement in the affair, Doc was intrigued and asked to interview the man's daughters, and although Melling was unwilling to comply, he did hand over a sketch of the creature that June had drawn following the encounter. The figure in the illustration was winged but had a humanlike body and sturdy legs. The head and face appeared unnatural with a gaping black mouth, large eyes, and pointy ears.

Descriptions of the incident, along with June Melling's sketch, appeared in print shortly thereafter, and just a few weeks later, two other young females apparently had a scary encounter with the Owlman in the same area. On July 3, Sally Chapman and Barbara Perry, both fourteen years of age, were camping in the woods near the church. As they settled down to make a kettle of tea just before 10:00 p.m., the girls were startled by a long, drawn-out hissing sound. Just then they noticed the apparition standing about twenty yards away. For what seemed to be an eternity, Sally and Barbara stared at the creature, and to their great dismay, it was staring right back at them! As the girls watched in utter amazement, the monster rose up straight off of the ground and disappeared into the treetops.

My good friend and colleague Jonathan Downes has written the quintessential book on the subject of Owlman. In 2001, he received an e-mail from a woman claiming to be Sally Chapman (apparently a pseudonym), who was looking to tell her side of the story after twenty-five years:

I had been to see a horror film…a few months before, a werewolf film…This was the first thing I thought when I saw it. I thought it was the werewolf. The face wasn't really like an owl, thinking back. It was like a frowning, sneering black thing. The eyes were burning, glaring and reddish. I don't know if it had fur or feathers, but it was gray and grizzled like the werewolf in the film. I remember hearing Barbara start to laugh, but it was a sort of a choked, panicked laugh…I knew right away it was REAL. It wasn't like a monster in the films that look rubbery and fake. It just looked like a very weird, frightening animal, as real as any animal in a zoo. It looked flesh and blood to me, but there is simply no way it could have been. It couldn't have been something that born and grew. No way. I have no idea what it was. My head even hurts thinking about it.

It was more frightening than I can really describe…It just stood there for what might have been a minute. I'm not really sure how long. Barbara was laughing, but it was more like a sort of breathless hysterical sound by now. I wanted to run but couldn't. It was so EVIL, intensely so. When it moved…its arms or wings or whatever went out, and it just rose up through the trees. Straight up through the evergreens, it didn't flap, it didn't make a sound. Then, weirdly, I thought "costume" for the first time, because the legs looked wrong. They looked like a kind of grey trouser material, certainly unnatural…And the feet. Black, hooking things. I have no idea how it had managed to stand up on them. They were like an earwig's tail-piece…I don't know how it could have disappeared like it did. The woods weren't that thick. Not thick enough to hide what I can only think of as a monster…It seemed to vanish, like a ghost.

Sally and Barbara fled the immediate area, though it was too dark outside to return home, so the terrified girls made camp at a thinner part of the forest until daylight. It must have been a long and sleepless night, as every noise in the dry, crunchy forest surrounding them caused their hearts to skip a beat. When daylight finally broke, the young girls wandered down to Grebe Beach and happened upon Doc Shiels, who listened with concern to their chilling tale. He separated Sally and Barbara and had them both draw sketches of the thing they had seen. The images looked strikingly similar to the creature drawn by June Melling.

At or around the time this was taking place, two other sisters with the last name of Greenwood claimed that they, too, spotted the Owlman as he was perching in the vicinity of Mawnan Church. In a letter to a local newspaper, Jane Greenwood stated, "It was standing in the trees like a full-grown man, but the legs bent backwards like a bird's. It saw us and quickly jumped up and rose straight up through the trees. My sister and I saw it very closely before it rose up. It has red slanting eyes and a very large mouth. The feathers are silvery grey and so are his body and legs. The feet are like a big, black crab's claws. We were frightened at the time. It was so strange, like something out of a horror film. We really saw the birdman…But how could it rise up like that? If we imagined it, then we both imagined it at the same time."

Owlman apparently took a two-year holiday, but reports began to surface again in 1978. According to an article that

Doc Shiels penned for *Fortean Times Magazine,* a sixteen-year-old female caught a glimpse of a "flying devil" near Mawnan Church on June 4 of that year, and a trio of French schoolgirls claimed they observed the monster on August 2. The students portrayed the entity as "a great big furry bird…white with a gaping mouth and big red eyes." The girls had first noticed the thing high up in the treetops and watched as it took off and flew out of sight. For years, many felt that Doc Shiels had conjured up the entire Owlman affair for his own amusement. But a corroborating report from the 1980s was uncovered because of diligent research by Jon Downes.

The primary eyewitness is a younger gentleman whom Jon has given the name "Gavin," since the man feels that going public could damage his professional reputation. But Downes has gotten to know Gavin quite well and is quite convinced by his testimony with regard to what he alleges he saw.

The event took place during the summer of 1988 or 1989 when Gavin was a young teen. It just so happened that he was vacationing in Cornwall with the family of his girlfriend at the time. The couple was taking an evening stroll down the lanes that circled about the groves of Mawnan Church. As the beam of Gavin's flashlight shone onto the robust branch of a tree about fifteen feet off the ground, it revealed the Owlman roosted upon it. The uncanny being seemed surprised by the sudden intrusion and jerked its head downward as it raised up its great wings in front. Within an instant, the thing had catapulted off its perch and disappeared behind the dense foliage.

In a prolonged interview with Downes, Gavin recalled the following details:

It was similar to a man in shape, and about four or four and a half feet high. It was grey, and with a texture like that on a bird with soft feathers ... The torch caught the eyes so they were reflected in the light and were bright yellowy, I think. It had a torso like a man, but had legs which were in proportion to its body, again similar to a man ... The feet were black and looked like pincers ... About halfway up the legs was an ankle with the legs bending back, with no visible knee like a person's knee. The torso would have been spindle shaped; broad at the top and at the bottom, so that it tapers towards the legs and went straight down. The head was really odd shaped. A really flat face, without any real outstanding features like an animal with a snout or anything. It had a black mouth curling down quite sharply at the corners, like an inverted "V," and with no other features on the face apart from the eyes really ... The top of the head was pointed and it had flaps at the side of the head about the same level as the eyes ... It had quite large arms, or wings, with long feathers.

Similar to most flying humanoid witnesses, the experience changed Gavin's life in a very dramatic way. He has apparently had ongoing nightmares and a constant sense of dread in the years following his sighting. The fact that as a budding naturalist he was familiar with owls and other birds seems to discount the possibility that he simply observed something common that evening. Throughout the years, there have been other vague reports of the Owlman stalking the woods and graveyard around Mawnan Church, but these accounts seem shrouded in ambiguity. Still, the Owlman seems to have left his indelible mark on many.

Maryland's Monsters

Across the United States, there are copious, colorful urban legends that depict a variety of whimsical hobgoblins. One such tale tells of Maryland's Snallygaster, typically conveyed as a giant winged creature with an elongated beak and, curiously, one prominent cyclopean eye resting in the center of its forehead. During the year 1909, newspapers around Maryland were abuzz with stories about the sinister Snallygaster and its daily dalliances. The Old Line State is also home to a number of other uncanny creatures, including the Sykesville Monster and something known as the Goat Man. Additionally, in an old issue of *Fate Magazine*, there is an obscure reference to a flying beast that was encountered by a Maryland man named John Kuluk sometime during the 1970s. Kuluk characterized the thing he saw as approximating a winged entity with a human face and no beak.

According to his description, the creature had gray feathers engulfing its body, especially its arms.

Years later, Mrs. Ruth Lundy of Woodbine, Maryland, wrote a letter to editor Mark Chorvinksy of *Strange Magazine*, detailing a flying humanoid she sighted in 1980:

> Mine was about ten years ago, when I was returning home around 3 a.m. after being out with a few friends to an all-night restaurant to eat. I was turning off 140 onto 91 in Finksburg, in Carroll County, Maryland, which at that time was not developed as it is now. The area was a high bank with a big cornfield at that time, which was used for farming. The field backed up to a Jewish graveyard. After I made that turn, I saw what I thought was a man. As I got closer, I saw what reminded me of a big pterodactyl-type thing, but standing on two feet like a man. The strange figure was brownish-gray and over six feet tall. The face of this figure was of a man, but the chin seemed to be pointed like a beak.
>
> The figure then started moving and, when it did, it looked as though it had wings, and the closer I got the faster it would flap its wings. It had a big wing span. The thing flew away. It flew over my car and the force of the wind made my whole car shake. The sound that wind made sounded almost like a helicopter. Driving towards it must have scared it. When I used to tell people about this, they thought I was putting them on but it's something I will never forget and even now, when I go through that area, even knowing how developed it is, I feel scared…

Taking it all into account, we must list the state of Maryland as one of those places where eerie, winged, humanlike things go bump in the night.

The Birdman
in the Graveyard

The following chapters will reveal that the nation of Mexico is ground zero for the flying humanoid phenomenon. But just prior to the start of the twenty-first century, there were apparently two intriguing chance encounters within the city of Monterrey. They would be the first of many. The initial sighting, which happened on the hot summer day of July 20, 1994, confirmed the fact that the subject in question was quite literally a hybrid between a bird and a man. Immediately before lunchtime, as he was walking past a graveyard, a farm laborer from Rancho El Sabino observed the chimera-like creature as it strutted "chickenlike" down an adjacent trail a considerable distance away. The thing extended its huge wings as it turned and disappeared out of sight. The awestruck ranch hand was not about to decipher where the monster had gone. Still, the terrified worker was able to identify the fact that the being was humanlike from its head down to its torso, though decidedly birdlike below its midriff, where it sported gray feathers and talons. Just a few days later, a bereaved woman who was visiting a gravesite spotted the very same entity and contacted local officials. The graveyard was subsequently investigated by a team of UFO researchers, though they were not able to reach any conclusions.

———————

The flock of bizarre birdmen that we have examined in this chapter may only scratch the surface, since most people are understandably hesitant to discuss these types of encounters. For not only are these allegations viewed as being utterly absurd, but they also seem to be associated with bad fortune and even death.

Case in point, former editor of *Strange Magazine* Mark Chorvinsky interviewed multiple witnesses who had reported seeing something he called the Potomac Mothman—a winged Michigan entity that made an appearance on July 27, 1944. Sadly, Chorvinsky surrendered to cancer at the premature age of fifty-one before he could dig deeper into the mystery.

I've also found an obscure reference to a South African creature referred to as the Albertville Man-Bird. A man named Farred Hoosin claimed to have had a sighting near Johannesburg in 1980. Hoosin described the apparition as "a dark-colored, birdlike figure."

Yet another flying humanoid was encountered at Kostroma, Russia, in 1990. An astonished crowd that had gathered to watch it gasped and pointed at the thing, which displayed large, gray wings, a flat face, and no neck whatsoever. A shadow was cast over its face, according to an eyewitness named Yuri M, who watched it fly at around speeds of thirty-five miles per hour.

Equally as puzzling as this global collection of winged humanoids is the menagerie of baffling beasties that combine the features of terrestrial animals with unnatural winglike appendages. We shall put them under the microscope in the following chapter.

FOUR

Gargoyles and Chimeras

Throughout the Old World, effigies of all manner of fanciful beasts were erected as stone monuments at a time when the world was dark and mysterious still. These spectacular gargoyles were particularly prominent on cathedrals, palaces, and other structures that were meant to denote spirituality and power. While some of these symbolic statues displayed the physical characteristics of known animals, such as dogs, lions, eagles, or even serpents, oftentimes there were unexpected features attached. Many of these chimerical hybrids included a highly significant and unexpected peculiarity: wings. While the reasons for including such appendages on these creature icons is purely speculative, there seem to be parallels to the flying humanoid problem. Humans are, after all, a distinct species, the product of a selective process of evolution that determines how a life-form gets around based on its environment and primary source of sustenance.

The order, which is comprised of bats (Chiroptera), is similarly unique. These highly specialized animals have found their niche in virtually every habitat on the planet. Their delicate airfoils are constructed of a thin membrane that is stretched across their elongated hands and fingers. But they are the only mammals with true wings. Scientifically speaking, the notion of any terrestrial mammal sprouting wings defies all reason. Yet such profoundly unnatural creatures have been documented, and the similarities to their equally perplexing man-bird cousins are noteworthy. In this chapter, I will highlight some winged monsters with markedly animalistic tendencies to see how they compare.

Jersey Devil

When we think of New Jersey, we typically picture bustling, overcrowded cities surrounded by factories and traffic-packed toll roads. But there is a reason it is known as the Garden State, which becomes clearly evident as one travels from the thriving metropolis of the northeast to the west and south. Vast areas of farmland and green foliage abound once one exits the urban sprawl, and there are still many tracts that remain as pristine today as they were in centuries past.

One such region is known as the Pine Barrens. Encompassing an area of over 2,200 square miles, it lies in the southeastern part of the state and remains largely unpopulated due to its dry and acidic soil, which is not conducive to agricultural development (despite the fact that it is dense with conifer trees and other plant life). Like most remote and uninhabited ranges, the Barrens are also steeped in mystery, with many colorful stories about its history and lore. Without a doubt, the most celebrated local legend pertains to the capricious monster known as the Jersey Devil.

While there are various eclectic parables about the creature's origin, the most widely accepted story dates back to the year 1735 and revolves around an alleged curse. It is said that at that time, there was an impoverished woman known as Mother Leeds (or perhaps Mother Shourds), who, upon learning that she was going to give birth to her thirteenth child, uttered an imprecation that caused her infant to take the form of a devilish beast. As an angry storm vacillated outside her tiny cabin, the demon emerged from her womb, sprouted wings, and shot out through her chimney in plain view of the horrified midwives who were in attendance. The Jersey Devil was thus spawned. In some versions of the fable, Mother Leeds was known to have willfully engaged in sorcery, while in others, the monster was the result of being born out of wedlock. Regardless, the abomination flew into the New Jersey wilderness where some believe it still exists today.

The generally agreed-upon appearance of the Jersey Devil includes a mixture of diverse animal features. Standing about three and a half feet tall, it is said to have the muzzle of a dog attached to a long, horselike head. Some accounts include curled ram's horns and eyes that glow like charcoal embers. Its long neck extends down to a body that most resembles a kangaroo's with thin, leathery bat wings sprouting from its back. Its fore limbs are diminutive and terminate in claws, and its lanky rear limbs sport hooves. It also possesses a serpentlike or ratlike tail with a fork on the end.

Like most flying monsters, the Jersey Devil's presence is greatly feared since it is viewed as a harbinger of death or some other impending disaster. It is believed that a clergyman banished the creature for a century beginning in 1740 but that the Devil returned right on schedule, making sporadic appearances throughout the Pine Barrens in the nineteenth century. Yet the period that represents the zenith of activity was the third week of January 1909.

Rumors of Devil sightings had first surfaced in the community of Woodbury, but just across the Delaware River in Bristol, Pennsylvania, residents awoke one morning to find hundreds of unidentified tracks sprawling across their lawns. The impressions most resembled a horse's hoof prints, but were discovered in highly unexpected places including roof-tops. In many instances, they stopped abruptly, as if whatever had made them had suddenly taken to the air.

On the evening of January 16, local Postmaster E. W. Minster happened to peer out his window and spotted the culprit flying over the river. According to Minster, the weird animal emitted a dull glow and let out a blood-curdling shriek as it flew past. Supposedly, other citizens including a police officer had also heard and spotted the winged specter earlier that same evening. Its cry was described as eerie and mournful, seemingly supernatural. The next day, events quickly shifted back across the river to New Jersey soil and specifically Burlington Township, where many more tracks and sightings were logged. It wasn't long before mass hysteria broke out across the state.

Just after 2:00 a.m. on January 19, a Gloucester City paper-hanger named Nelson Evans, along with his wife, had the most lengthy sighting of the Devil. The couple claimed that they had been alerted to a dreadful sound and when they glanced out their window, they spotted the winged apparition cavorting about on the roof of their shed for over ten minutes. The thing's appearance was utterly grotesque, and when they couldn't stomach its presence any longer, Mr. Evans opened the window and shouted, "Shoo." This seems to have done the trick, since the Devil turned its head and "barked" at them both before departing in an abrupt manner.

The following day, an extensive account of the Evans'
sighting appeared in the *Philadelphia Evening Bulletin* along
with an artist's interpretation of the creature they had seen.
The sketch ended up becoming the enduring image of the
Jersey Devil that most people are familiar with to this day.
Sightings of the monster, which was now also being referred
to as a Jabberwock, continued for a few more days as the
Devil zigzagged across the region, creating a general sense of
panic among the populace.

Newspapers of the time chronicled the beast's escapades
as it gallivanted from town to town during its weeklong reign
of terror. A trolley full of passengers was dive-bombed by
the Devil in Haddon Heights on January 21. The conduc-
tor, a gentleman with the name of Lewis Boeger, stated that
the animal was hideous and displayed the general form of
a flying kangaroo with a long neck. Next, Daniel Flynn of
Leiperville, Pennsylvania, spotted the Devil as he was walking to work one day and described the monstrosity as man-
sized with a scaly hide like an alligator. A Mrs. Sorbinski of
Camden, New Jersey, apparently watched in horror as the
creature attacked her dog, causing it serious injury. Another
woman in Philadelphia was confronted by the Devil as she
collected her laundry. She claimed that it had spewed flames
out of its mouth. The abomination was even accused of
melting twenty feet of railroad tracks by an employee who
watched it perform the destructive deed. Other places where
the Jersey Devil was seen included Burlington, Trenton,

Pemberton, Moorestown, Collingswood, Riverside, Swedesboro, and Glassboro. Calling cards attributed to the Jersey Devil included numerous tracks and the remains of small animals it had devoured.

By February of 1909, the sightings seemed to have ceased. Explanations of the Jersey Devil's true identity were put forward by unnamed sources claiming to be scientists and experts on the subject. The most prevalent theory stated that the creature was something prehistoric in nature, perhaps hidden from mankind for millions of years until it had somehow managed to escape the confines of the underground caverns where it had been imprisoned. At one point, two enterprising gentlemen surfaced, claiming that they had in fact managed to capture the beast. The specimen could be viewed for a small fee, but it was quickly revealed to be a painted kangaroo with fake wings glued to its back.

In retrospect, the entire 1909 affair may have been a massive real estate hoax, an elaborate fabrication intended to force distraught homeowners to sell their property at reduced prices. Events were likely escalated by newspaper publishers looking to capitalize on the rumors. It is widely believed that many of the tracks attributed to the Jersey Devil were manufactured by artificial means and that the sightings were fictional. Consequently, there have not been many reports chronicled in the last century.

A brief resurgence did occur in 1930 when two men from Erial, New Jersey, encountered a being with "the body of a man, head of a cow, large bat wings and big feet." The eye-witnesses, Howard Marcey and John Huntzinger, claimed they watched the critter fly up into the air and over the tree-tops. Marcey's young sister also saw the thing the very next day. Well over two decades later, in 1952, some unidentified animal tracks were found in the snow on a Pine Barrens farm, but they were quickly determined to have been faked.

People frequently ask me what I really think of the Jersey Devil and I have always responded that it has all of the markings of an ostentatious urban legend, since no real animal could possibly account for the nonsensical descriptions. However, a report that I received from a gentleman named Johnathan Lackey has caused me to somewhat reluctantly reconsider my position on the matter. Throughout the course of multiple e-mails and phone interviews with me, Mr. Lackey has laid out a pretty amazing scenario, whereby he and another witness encountered a gargoyle-like beast near the Delaware River back in the summer of 1977.

At the time, Johnathan and his friend Bill were teenagers, cruising along Route 32 on the wooded outskirts of Yardley, Pennsylvania. The youths had acquired a 40,000-lumens spotlight and were trying it out by shining it on the road ahead of them. Johnathan admitted to me that he had been interested in animal mysteries since he was a young boy. In fact, he considered himself to be somewhat of a bookworm and natural history enthusiast while growing up. But he certainly never expected to run into a totally unknown species.

As the boys came over one particular hill, they lit up something that was standing in the road.

Johnathan's first impression of the subject was that the general shape of its body resembled that of a large dog like a Doberman. The creature displayed the tawny color of a deer and had four long, thin legs. But in the glare of the powerful spotlight, he could see that the specimen also possessed huge feathered wings that it held in an upright position, in addition to a prehensile tail. The animal's black face and head hair reminded Johnathan of a squirrel monkey, and it appeared to be soaking wet, as if it had been swimming in the adjacent Delaware River. The thing had pointy ears "like batman" that stood straight up on top of its head. Johnathan had a good enough look that he was able to discern other details, such as the fact that the critter had a short neck and a deep chest, which sloped upward to its small waist. Its paws appeared to be charcoal in color, as was the tip of its tail. As Johnathan and his companion Bill watched in wonder, the animal jumped from the middle of the road and glided down a hill out of sight.

The young men immediately turned to each other in disbelief and agreed that they had both seen something beyond explanation. Johnathan confided in me that for years he did not like to discuss the incident with anyone else for fear of being ridiculed but that he had reached a point in his life where he didn't care what people thought about him. *"I know what I saw!"* he emphatically stated to me during one conversation. Whatever Johnathan and his friend Bill encountered on that memorable night in the 1970s, it seems to fit the profile of the Jersey Devil better than anything else I am aware of.

"Jersey Devil Sketch" © Jonathan Lackey

Brentford Griffin

The notion of a four-legged animal with wings is contrary to everything we know about the nature of evolution. Though we do find mythological creatures that fit this profile quite handsomely. Case in point, the fabulous griffin, which combines the body of a lion with the wings (and sometimes the head) of an eagle. Heraldic images and related legends about these majestic creatures can be found in distant and varied places, including Ancient Greece, North Africa, and throughout parts of Europe.

Griffins were deemed to be fierce guardians. Their presence typically marked places of great importance, including hidden treasure-filled vaults and royal tombs. In the British Isles, griffin imagery adorns many coats of arms, symbolizing mighty power.

The West London suburb of Brentford seems to possess an uncanny connection to these chimeras. And in the years 1984 and 1985, this seemingly ordinary community may have even been visited by one of these legendary beasts.

The strange saga was brought to the public's attention by the local media. The primary eyewitness was a twenty-eight-year-old telephone technician by the name of Kevin Chippendale. As it turns out, Chippendale claims to have had two independent sightings of the creature months apart, though strangely in the same exact location and under identical circumstances. On both occasions, Chippendale had left his house on Brooke Road South on foot and was strolling down adjacent Braemar Road when he happened to glance up and see the strange animal flying over. It appeared to be hundreds of feet up in the air and was passing in front of some tall apartment buildings known ironically as the Green Dragon Towers. In an interview with Brentford Griffin researcher and author Andrew Collins, Chippendale presented an intriguing description.

Collins wrote, "The beast's size was difficult to determine. It was possibly the size of 'a large dog,' maybe even larger. It had four legs and what appeared to be paws. There was no beak, although Kevin did emphasize its muzzle-like nose. Its skin surface seemed 'smooth,' not feathery, and it did look aerodynamic, despite its apparent performance. However, the wings did not seem to be flapping like those of a normal bird in flight. They were much slower, almost as if they were moving in slow motion." He summarized by noting, "Not much more was noticed, other than Kevin's belief that he may have seen eyes and a tail of some description."

Chippendale confessed to Collins that at first he had been afraid to discuss the matter with anyone else for fear of appearing "unbalanced," though he eventually did confide in his family members. The utterly weird part is that Brentford's professional football club plays on a pitch known as Griffin Stadium, and the city also sports two griffins on its coat of arms, which was conceived back in 1932. In fact, Chippendale had passed a pub called The Griffin Brewery just minutes before each of his sightings. Curiously, the establishment bears the image of one of the creatures on its sign.

Skeptics would be quick to point out that Chippendale was predisposed to the power of suggestion, resulting in some kind of hallucination or even an outright lie. But there appears to have been other residents who encountered the monstrosity, too.

One of Chippendale's co-workers, a woman named Angela Keyhoe, told him that she had spotted a gigantic winged animal perched on top of a Brentwood landmark known as the gasworks, an enormous utility tank. At the time, she was seated on the top level of a double-decker bus, and evidently other passengers saw it, too. Angela's excitement was apparent to local arts center workers whom she had informed immediately after the incident. There was also a psychologist named John Olssen who came forward, stating that he had seen an enormous birdlike thing while jogging along the Thames River early one morning.

Publicity generated by the local press resulted in the forming of a griffin-spotting club and at least one other report. Though some residents pointed to a local author named Robert Rankin as the source of the confusion. Rankin had organized a UFO symposium at the town's arts center and had suggested that accounts of the Brentford Griffin could be traced back to the years prior to World War II, according to ambiguous sources. Sadly, the mythological visitor seems to have vacated the Brentford area in recent years.

Batsquatch

We couldn't possibly have a discussion about manlike monsters without mentioning the iconic, hulking, hairy manbeasts commonly referred to as Bigfoot or, frequently, as Sasquatch. Accounts of these legendary ape-men have existed in the Pacific Northwest for centuries, particularly in the piney forests surrounding Washington State's Mount Rainier. Its image is very familiar to us all—towering, hirsute, and presumably weighing several hundred pounds, certainly not the type of thing you would expect to see sailing through the air. Yet curiously, a singular incident might lead us to believe otherwise.

At 9:30 on the evening of Saturday, April 16, 1994, an eighteen-year-old student named Brian Canfield was driving his pickup truck southeast of Buckley, Washington, in the shadow of Mount Rainier. Brian was headed to a remote settlement known as Camp One, which lies adjacent to Lake Kapowsin. Without warning, his headlights suddenly dimmed and the engine shut completely off. Brian found himself hopelessly stranded on the isolated road. Then, as if the situation were not bad enough, things took a terrifying turn when a gigantic creature began to descend from the sky, directly in front of his vehicle. The great beast landed on the pavement ahead of him.

Brian could hardly believe his eyes, as the monster stood at least nine feet tall and was extremely muscular with wings as wide as the road. In the dim moonlight, the nervous youth could make out its wolflike head with tremendous, white teeth and striking, triangular, yellow eyes with crescent-shaped pupils. The thing appeared to be covered in blue fur, and its hands and feet were clawed.

In Brian's estimation, the nightmarish ogre was merely resting, and Brian did not perceive it as being dangerous, though the young man did feel strangely out of place. After a couple of uncomfortable minutes, the monster turned around and began to flap its powerful wings, flying away into the night. A few moments after it had departed, Brian's car mysteriously came back to life, and he hightailed it home, bursting into his house in a state of panic and revealing the unbelievable event to his parents, who could see that he had been visibly shaken by something.

Brian's father was moved by his son's apprehension and returned with him to the scene, but they could find no sign of the creature. A resulting investigation by police and reporters seemed to support the fact that Brian had a reputation as a clean and sober, upstanding student who had never been in trouble or prone to flights of fancy. One of Brian's friends coined the name "Batsquatch," based on its similarities to the hairy giant, and the name stuck.

As far as we know, there has never been another sighting of the creature. I cannot help but to wonder if there is a connection to the UFOs observed over Mount Rainier mentioned in chapter two. After all, Brian's creature certainly doesn't jive with anything we are familiar with on Earth.

Chilean Chupacabras

In 1995, a new breed of monster burst onto the scene. Its manifestation was prefaced by a flurry of livestock mutilations on the Caribbean island nation of Puerto Rico. Most disturbing was the fact that the animal corpses, which included goats, sheep, chickens, and rabbits, were reported to be completely devoid of blood, as if some modern vampire had paid them a visit in the dark of night. Allegedly, two telltale puncture wounds were the only sign left behind by the unseen attacker. Soon, reports of hideous, goblinlike creatures with large, lidless eyes and razor-sharp claws began to surface. The Chupacabra ("goat sucker") had arrived.

Over the next few years, the sightings spread throughout Latin America to countries that included Mexico and Nicaragua. And following the turn of the century, the focus shifted to the South American nation of Chile. Specifically, to the barren, desert region in the north, where farm animals began to fall victim en masse.

One of the very first Chupacabra encounters took place around 8:00 p.m. on April 29, 2000. A farm laborer named Jose Ismael Pino was searching for an escaped bull when instead he came upon a four-foot-tall creature that resembled a winged monkey with protruding fangs and long arms that terminated in clawed hands. Pino unleashed a pack of hunting dogs on the entity, resulting in an unfortunate outcome for at least one of the dogs.

Four years later in July of 2004, Juan Acuqa from the city of Parral claimed he was attacked by two unidentified animals at 2:00 a.m. one Sunday. Following the traumatic incident, Acuqa told reporters, "They were dog-faced and had wings. This isn't a normal situation, I told myself." Evidently not, since the things were overpowering the poor man the entire time in an apparent attempt to chew off his face, though one of them did manage to bite him on the leg and rip his clothes. Acuqa escaped by jumping into a canal and swimming to his brother-in-law's house. He was subsequently rushed to a local hospital where physicians noted defensive injuries on his arms, shoulders, and back. The local district attorney later determined that the wounds could not have been made by a person.

Then, just a few weeks later, there was a much-publicized case that transpired in the remote Pampa Acha region. The Abett de la Torre Diaz family was motoring toward Arica at around 11:00 p.m. when they sighted several creatures they characterized as "dog-faced kangaroos" leaping through the air. The father, Carlos, was known as an army sub-officer with an outstanding reputation. He later stated that the animals had essentially looked like gargoyles. Carlos explained, "I was sitting in the backseat with my brothers, talking, and suddenly everything went dark. Then I told my brother what I was seeing and he told me to keep quiet because Mom gets nervous. Later I looked through the window and saw some things that looked like birds, with dog's heads and backswept wings."

Carlos's wife, Teresa, was sitting in the front seat and had the best view of the mystifying critters as they drew closer. She observed four of the things prancing in the moonlight and noted how the subjects appeared to be moving in slow motion, despite the fact that they were easily keeping pace with the speeding automobile. After ten minutes of stunned silence, the family decided to discuss the matter but couldn't come to any conclusions about what they had seen. But once they arrived at their destination, they did become quite apprehensive about the return trip home. According to some Chilean UFO researchers, the same or similar animals had also been sighted by a different car full of witnesses just a few days earlier.

Briggs Road Man Bat

Author and researcher Linda Godfrey has investigated all manner of eclectic creatures in her home state of Wisconsin, including reports of menacing beasts that are described as veritable, modern-day werewolves. Yet one of the more macabre entities that she has tackled is undoubtedly something known as the Man Bat of Briggs Road. As a high-profile personality, Godfrey is a conduit for all sorts of strange happenings in her neck of the woods, and it is for this reason that one particular gentleman got in touch with her. The fifty-three-year-old's name is Wohali, and he is of Cherokee descent. He and his twenty-five-year-old son were driving home from La Crosse, Wisconsin in their pickup truck just after 9:00 the evening of September 26, 2006. As they neared their hometown of Holmen, the men rounded a hill near a wooded area on Briggs Road. That's when they were apparently divebombed by an animal far beyond their comprehension.

The brownish-gray, fleshy monster was at least six feet tall in their estimation and had leathery wings that seemed to span half the road, perhaps stretching fourteen feet across. The thing also had a noticeably protruding rib cage and manlike legs with clawed talons. Yet the most unnerving aspect was surely its diabolical face, which featured reflective yellow eyes and a toothy grimace. The Man Bat reminded them both of a vampire from a Hollywood movie.

Both witnesses got the distinct impression that the apparition was not merely popping in to exchange pleasantries. After a scary moment when the demon seemed intent on smashing right through their windshield, it suddenly veered off and shot up into the treetops at incredible speed. "I've never seen anything move like that," Wohali later remarked.

As it departed, the Man Bat uttered a bone-chilling shriek that seemed to trigger a response in both men, as they became violently ill and had to pull over to the side of the road. A high-pitched wringing sound lingered in their heads. Wohali did not feel well for days following the incident and both he and his son wondered if they had encountered something supernatural, since their home was subsequently plagued by strange noises and an eerie vibe that caused their dog to take refuge under the bed.

The Man Bat is not the only winged weirdo from Wisconsin, since there are also accounts of something called the Reptile Man of Route 13 (located south of Medford). This being was encountered at least two times during the 1990s, once by a state official and shortly thereafter by a truckload of highway workers. All who spotted it declared it to be a scaly, green, lizardlike humanoid with sprawling bat wings attached to its back. The state official had watched it shoot straight up into the air in front of him and then descend vertically behind him in an unbelievable fashion.

Britain's Bat—Winged Monkey Bird

Our next creature arrives courtesy of cryptozoologist Karl Shuker, who was presented with a testimonial from a British woman named Jacki Hartley. Shuker subsequently wrote an article for *Beyond Magazine* in 2008 that highlighted her strange sightings of a creature that seems to display the attributes of no less than three different animals. Ms. Hartley claims to have had three separate encounters with the mind-baffling chimera at different locales throughout Great Britain, beginning in 1969 at age four. According to Jacki's original correspondence, "I was in the back of the car when I suddenly heard an awful screeching scream. Mum and dad were in the front chatting and heard nothing. It was twilight and as I looked out the back window into the trees, I saw what I can only describe as a monster. It had bat wings which it unfolded and stretched out before folding back up again, red eyes and a kind of monster monkey face with a parrot's beak and was about three feet in height."

Jacki further insisted that she spotted the thing once again when she was eleven years old, as her family was motoring near the village of Robertsbridge. Her most recent encounter was in October of 2006, when she caught a glimpse of the animal sailing past the window of her home in Tunbridge.

One must acknowledge the obvious in recognizing that as the sole eyewitness of this entity, Jacki may have been experiencing something both personal and supernatural in nature. In one e-mail to Shuker, she acknowledged this fact: "Although the creature looked solid flesh and blood and made an awful sound, I think it could be paranormal in origin as I have never seen or read about anything that even vaguely resembles it." Furthermore, Jacki was plagued with nightmares featuring the monster for weeks following her initial sighting. In his article, Shuker points out the obvious similarities between the Bat-Winged Monkey Bird and its British counterpart, the Owlman, though in many ways, this quirky dervish belongs in a category all its own.

Gargoyles are Bigger in Texas

In *Monsters of Texas,* my co-author Nick Redfern and I wrote about two different instances where winged, gargoyle-like creatures allegedly scared the wits out of residents in the state's dusty Panhandle region.

The first story was related to Redfern by an elderly couple in 2001. Littlefield is a small, isolated farming community that lies just northwest of Lubbock. Old-timers in town often reminisce about a spooky, broken-down ranch house that once rested on the outskirts of town. Back in 1946, the domicile was apparently owned by a pair of rarely seen, senile sisters who kept to themselves. During that particular year, a group of curious teenagers were poking mischievously around the property on a dare one fateful night when the wooden cellar doors adjacent to the farmhouse flew open. In plain view of all who were present, a pair of gray, winged humanoids with blood-red eyes emerged from the opening. Most remarkable of all, the beings appeared to stand no less than eight feet tall! Before the slack-jawed teenagers could make their hasty retreat, they watched as the giants shuffled around for a few minutes before spreading their great wings and flying off into the starlit sky. The couple also informed Redfern that many of those who had witnessed the event ended up dying under unusual circumstances.

One hundred miles to the east of Littlefield is the tiny hamlet of Dickens, which claims a population of just over three hundred people. In 2006, something resembling a winged goblin was encountered there one night by a female student who was driving south on Highway 70 at a place called Turkey Crossing. According to a letter that the young woman's mother submitted to cryptozoologist Craig Woolheater:

> She [the daughter] noticed that there was something sitting on a wide gate post. She did not know what it was so she slowed down to look. As she got closer, she saw a flesh-colored animal, about three feet tall, crouched on top of the post. It had a round head like an owl and a round, sloped face with a tiny round nose, like a short snout and a slit for the mouth. It had eyes that looked like they were slanted down. The creature was sitting with its feet together and its knees out, in a bow-legged squat. It had feet like a bird with a set of toes or talons in the back and another set in the front. It had short arms with a flap of triangular skin on the backsides. There was something pointed to the tips of the skin flaps that looked like a thumb or claw. It look like it had paws with four digits on each one and the arms were partially hidden underneath a flap of skin on each side. The skin or short fur was a tan or peach color and it was wrinkled in places like a baby bat.

As the student watched in disbelief, the weird little creature pounced off of its perch and landed in the road, causing her to swerve to avoid hitting it. It crouched down menacingly for a brief moment and then started to run away as the terrified witness sped off in a state of hysterics. When she arrived home a short time later, the girl broke down in front of her mother, who was alarmed by her daughter's level of fear. This was evidently the mother's motivation in writing her letter to Craig Woolheater.

Texas seems to be home to many types of gargoyles. A business owner in San Antonio once told me that back in the 1970s, he remembered watching a television news story about a winged dog (similar to the Brentford Griffin) that had been observed prancing around on the roof of a house. Police officers were apparently called to the scene and fired upon the animal, though it managed to escape the flurry of bullets. We must truly wonder if Texas's close proximity to the nation of Mexico has a bearing on these remarkable events. For as we will learn in a subsequent chapter, that particular country holds many clues to the flying humanoid mystery.

The Bay Area's Bat Thing

One final chimera-like case we will examine unfolded in California's Bay Area in 1975, according to Fortean author Barton Nunnelly, who chronicles the episode in his thought-provoking book titled *The Inhumanoids*.

> Multiple witnesses claimed they saw a large "gargoyle" perched in a tree and later on the roof of a house in Walnut Creek, California in October. It was described as being humanoid with gray, wrinkled or leathery skin, and with an estimated wingspan of over fifteen feet! "It was so big

that it made the tree, which was about 100 feet high, look like a bush," claimed Lloyd King of Oakland. "It was at least five feet tall, had a head like a vulture, and big gray wings. It was so out of scale with the tree that I thought my eyes were playing tricks on me, so I got my kids and the neighbors, and we looked at it for about five minutes. It suddenly just glided off without flapping its huge wings…"

Nunnelly also references a second sighting of the creature whereby a custodian by the name of Minelli alleged to have stumbled upon the monster as he was taking out the trash one night. The gigantic thing had apparently assumed the posture of a gargoyle on an awning atop his building. Minelli summarized the incident by declaring, "It was such an impossibly monstrous thing. I was afraid to say anything about it because everybody would think I was crazy… It must have been a bird, unless it was the devil himself."

————————

As we can clearly see, so-called devils, griffins, and all manner of bat-winged boogeymen have been encountered in the Western Hemisphere over the last century. Yet none of these startling apparitions has quite captured the public's imagination like the king of all winged phantoms—West Virginia's mind-boggling Mothman!

FIVE

The Mothman Cometh

Mothman is one of the most enigmatic and notorious figures in the annals of the unexplained. A gray, manlike creature standing over six feet tall with immense wings attached to his body, Mothman represents a monster in the truest sense of the word. Most eyewitnesses have described it as possessing a low-slung head with two enormous eyes. And the most startling feature are the eyes: giant, blood-red embers like automobile reflectors that seemingly have a hypnotic power over humans. In some instances, motorists have claimed to have been chased by Mothman at speeds approaching one hundred miles per hour, despite the fact that the creature barely even flaps its wings when it flies.

These esoteric descriptions obviously don't match anything we are familiar with in the natural world. Seemingly stepping right out of a science fiction movie, Mothman's sole purpose seems to be to stalk and terrify humans, quite possibly leaving a wake of utter devastation in its path. In the pages that follow, I will attempt to shed some light on this complex and mystifying case.

"Mothman Rendering" © Ginger Bertline

The Quintessential Encounter

Point Pleasant, West Virginia, is a sleepy, rural town situated on the banks of the mighty Ohio River. This historic community was once the epicenter of intense Mothman hysteria that reached its peak a year before the tragic collapse of the Silver Bridge, which occurred on December 15, 1967, taking forty-six lives and propelling the community into the national spotlight. Yet to most, the episode actually began just before midnight on November 15, 1966, when two young couples were cruising the back roads of a local hangout known as the TNT Area, so named because it had served as an ammunitions production and storage facility during World War II. The wooded tract, which lies adjacent to the 25,000-acre McClintic Wildlife Management Area, is peppered with almost one hundred concrete igloos that have served to store explosives and other hazardous chemicals throughout the years. It's a creepy place.

Roger and Linda Scarberry and Steve and Mary Mallette were looking for some excitement as they drove the winding lanes of the desolate parcel that fateful evening. Ultimately, they would get far more than they had ever bargained for. As they motored past an abandoned building known as the power plant, the women both noticed a tall figure standing by the derelict structure. At first, the form appeared to resemble a towering man. Though, they were immediately mesmerized by the being's piercing, scarlet eyes, which were estimated to be two inches wide and six inches apart. To their extreme horror, the apparition began to shuffle awkwardly toward the entrance of the building, and it was then that they got a good look at it. Despite the fact that its body and legs were muscular and humanlike, the being did not have any visible arms or even a perceptible head, although two large wings folded high against its back were readily apparent. According to Roger, the thing had appeared to stand between six and seven feet tall.

At this point, the group was understandably in hysterics. Roger pushed the accelerator to the floor of his '57 Chevy and tore down the exit road toward the adjacent Highway 63. But to their utter shock and dismay, the uncanny creature reappeared ahead of them on a hill and immediately took flight, shooting straight up in the air like a helicopter.

As they sped south towards Point Pleasant, the Mothman was in hot pursuit, apparently gliding just above and behind their vehicle. Mary Mallette, who was sitting in the backseat, claimed that she could hear the monster making a glirine, squeaking sound. Although it did not seem to flap its ten-foot-long wings, Mothman easily kept pace with the car, despite speeds approaching the century mark. At the edge of town it suddenly vanished.

The frazzled group pulled into a local drive-in restaurant in order to discuss what to do next. Linda thought they should report the incident to the local police, but they were all worried that they would not be believed. After some debate, both couples decided to drive back to the location of the sighting to see if they could spot the creature again, and much to their dismay, they did indeed see it standing in a farmer's pasture right outside of town. As they watched it, the thing stumbled clumsily into the darkness.

Now frantic, the Scarberrys and Mallettes raced into the Mason County Court House and filed a report with Deputy Millard Halstead, who was impressed by the sincerity and emotional state of the distraught witnesses. Point Pleasant is a close-knit community, and Halstead knew the young people to be respectable, law-abiding citizens who weren't prone to flights of fancy or deception. Eventually, when the group had mustered up the courage to return to the location where they had first observed the monster, they were reluctantly led back to the spot by Deputy Halstead. Once there, they perceived what they interpreted to be weird noises and detected shadowy movements and a mysterious dust cloud, none of which they were eager to investigate.

The very next morning, Sheriff George Johnson held a press conference detailing the encounter, and the unbelievable story was picked up by the local and national media. The press eventually dubbed the monster Mothman (based on a character from the *Batman* television series), and a modern legend was born.

It is worth noting that Linda Scarberry was apparently so shaken by the ordeal that she had to be taken to the hospital for treatment of shock shortly after the encounter. Haunted by her experience with Mothman, she and her husband Roger eventually moved back to live with her parents, and she later claimed that she subsequently endured many unexplained occurrences, including disembodied noises, disturbing phone calls, visits from intimidating Men in Black, and what she interpreted to be poltergeist activity whereby objects around her home seemed to move by themselves.

Unlike the others, who seemed eager to disassociate themselves from the encounter, Linda had the remarkable courage to speak publicly on many occasions about that fateful night, though her memories seemed to evolve a bit over the years. For example, in later interviews she claimed that one of Mothman's wings was actually caught in a guard wire when they had first spotted it and that the being was attempting to extricate itself with its two "arms." Linda also described Mothman as being flesh colored with angelic, white wings rather than the gray hue reported by virtually every other witness. During one interview, she even stated that she had seen the Mothman "hundreds of times." And during a comprehensive interview with Mothman Museum curator, researcher, and author Jeff Wamsley, Linda explained how she would frequently observe the creature around Point Pleasant on subsequent occasions.

We must wonder if her initial sighting left her emotionally scarred to the extent that she suffered severe posttraumatic stress and paranoia. Or does this phenomenon target specific individuals like a form of possession? Sadly, Linda Scarberry passed away on March 6, 2011, following a bout with cancer. Her companions on that fateful night seem to have long-since faded into ambiguity.

A Face—to—Face Confrontation

The night after the Scarberry/Mallette incident, hundreds of curious people prowled the TNT Area, hoping to catch a glimpse of the macabre visitor that had put in an appearance there. But it was an unsuspecting Point Pleasant resident named Marcella Bennett who got closer to Mothman than anyone ever has. Marcella and her three-year-old daughter, Tina, were traveling through the area, along with her younger brother, Raymond Wamsley (apparently no relation to Jeff), and his wife. Oblivious to the search that was going on in the nearby woods, the group was driving over to visit one of the only families that lived among the concrete storage igloos, the clan of Ralph Thomas.

Overhead, abstruse lights flickered in the night sky and caught the attention of Raymond, though he dismissed them as belonging to an airplane and forged ahead. When the group arrived at the secluded Thomas residence, they had learned that Ralph and his wife were not at home, though three of his children were there at the time. As they strolled back to their car, Raymond asked Marcella to look up and render an opinion on the unidentified lights he had spotted earlier. Anxious to get back to the vehicle, Marcella ignored his request and stumbled forward. As she reached down for the door handle, she caught sight of something looming out of the corner of her eye. It was the Mothman.

According to a 2003 interview with author and researcher Andy Colvin, Marcella was looking down and saw feet, which appeared abnormal. As she slowly raised her eyes, her mind attempted to make sense of what stood directly in front of her. The stunned Marcella at first thought it might be a man in a jumpsuit, perhaps some kind of worker. But to her horror, she quickly realized that whatever the six-foot-tall being was, it was not human.

Bennett recalled,

> At first, my first thought was, it's a guy. You know, it's a man. I could see it was gray. I kept thinking, gray, khaki work clothes ... and then ... okay ... feathers. I thought—Oh God! Feathers! Not a man! It was a man, but not a man of this Earth. I don't know what he was. He was shaped like a male. The huge wings. The way he was standing. The head like a bird. I'll never forget the way he was standing. It was like he was just relaxing. Like he was just waiting for that moment for me to walk up. The neck looked like it was hanging, on this side ... The neck looked like it went down in, like a bird. Way down in the neck. To me it wasn't of this world.

As Ray Wamsley and his wife yelled out and sprinted back to the safety of the Thomas home, Marcella turned to flee, and her legs literally gave out on her. She collapsed on the ground and fell directly on top of young Tina, who couldn't breathe: "I couldn't get up to get off of her and I thought, well you know, she's dead. I'm killing her. But I couldn't move. I was in a trance." For what seemed to be an eternity, Marcella lay paralyzed on top of her young child until she heard a sound, which she interpreted to be the flapping of enormous wings. Whatever the being was, it appeared to have departed.

When she was finally able to summon up the strength to get to her feet, Marcella scraped up poor Tina and made a mad dash to the Thomas household, where her companions had gained entrance by banging on the door until the children had answered their cries for help. While they locked the door behind them and began to phone the local police, one of the Thomas children peeked out the window and claimed that she saw the Mothman clambering onto their wooden porch. According to some accounts, the specter even peered into the window at the terrified witnesses. But by the time the police had arrived on the scene, the creature had apparently disappeared for good.

Like Linda Scarberry, Marcella Bennett was greatly traumatized by her experience. She had to seek medical attention for anxiety after the incident and apparently dealt with a lifetime of paranoia and nightmares. Oftentimes, in a conscious state, she would still sense the presence of the Mothman nearby and feel totally unnerved. Marcella confided in Andy Colvin that she felt as though her encounter had also led to psychic visions and premonitions, a belief apparently shared by other eyewitnesses. Like Linda Scarberry, Bennett passed away a few years ago.

Sheer Terror!

Following Marcella Bennett's close encounter, word of the Mothman obtained worldwide notoriety. Newspapers around the globe were publishing articles and editorials about the startling occurrences around Point Pleasant, and, as a result, the tiny community unwittingly found itself on the map. Many residents began to come forward with tales of their own Mothman sightings, in addition to rumors of UFOs flitting about in the night skies and also visits from mysterious and intimidating Men in Black, who would urge them not to talk about their sightings.

One particularly disturbing story was that of a young woman named Connie Jo Carpenter from New Haven, about thirteen miles northeast of Point Pleasant. At 10:30 the morning of Sunday, November 27, Connie was driving home from church alone when she noticed a statuesque figure standing on the side of the road, adjacent to the Mason County Golf Course. In her estimation, the thing appeared manlike, though it was massive, standing at least seven feet tall.

Suddenly and without warning, the being sprouted two great wings, and as Connie watched in disbelief, the entity took off straight up in the air, banking sharply and heading straight toward her car. Like other witnesses, she was mesmerized by its large red eyes, though she remembers its tiny face as looking "horrible ... like something out of a science fiction movie." As quickly as it had come into view, the Mothman departed, leaving distraught Connie in thorough disbelief. Almost immediately afterward, she developed a severe case of conjunctivitis. According to investigator and author John Keel, who interviewed her a short time later, Connie's eyes had looked extremely red and irritated, and she was left badly shaken by her encounter.

By the following February, Connie and her husband Keith had moved just across the river to Ohio, where a man in a vintage Buick attempted to abduct her one morning while she was walking to school. She managed to escape, but shortly thereafter she received a threatening note on her doorstep that essentially stated, "Watch yourself girl. We can get you." This event apparently pushed poor Connie over the edge, according to her now ex-husband Keith, who was interviewed in a documentary in 2002. Connie has apparently withdrawn from public life and refuses to talk about either event to this very day.

Mothman's influence was steadily spreading out from Point Pleasant, West Virginia, by late November of 1966 to the southeast in St. Albans, a suburb of Charleston. A woman named Ruth Foster apparently spotted the monster standing in her backyard one night. Mrs. Foster had heard her dog barking at 10:30 on the evening of November 26 and stepped out on her porch to investigate. She later recalled, "It was tall with big red eyes that popped out of its face … It had a funny little face. I didn't see any beak. All I saw were those big red poppy eyes. I screamed and ran back into the house. My brother-in-law went out to look, but it was gone."

The following evening, teenager Sheila Cane and her younger sister claimed that they were chased by the Mothman after they had stumbled upon the creature near a St. Albans dumpsite. Sheila summarized the chilling tale this way: "It was gray and white...and it must have been seven feet tall, taller than a man. I screamed and we ran home. It flew up in the air and followed us part of the way." The two youths further explained that the winged monster was beakless with "big, red pop-eyes."

Chasing teenagers seems to be one of Mothman's favorite pastimes. According to Faye DeWitt-Leport, she, along her brother and two younger siblings, had headed out to the TNT Area one night hoping to catch a glimpse of the creature. It is a fact of life that if we are not careful, sometimes we may actually find what we are looking for. As the youths drove through the location, her brother was the first to notice the horrific being standing off to the side of the road. The way Faye explains it, the Mothman was running alongside their car, peering in the window at them. When her brother quickly swerved and came to a stop, the monster actually dove onto the hood of their vehicle and then shot straight up in the air, finally perching (like a gargoyle) four stories up on the overhang of an abandoned building. As it hissed at them in a menacing fashion, Faye's brother began to hurl stones at the thing, despite her protests. Eventually, this seemed to irritate the creature to the extent that it assumed an aggressive posture that caused them all to flee the area.

Other Encounters

In the weeks following the initial encounters, newspapers from around the region published numerous articles about people claiming to have seen the enigmatic visitor.

A precursor to this incident with Faye may have transpired when a man named Kenneth Duncan was working at a cemetery in the town of Clendenin. He was digging a grave for his brother-in-law, along with four other men, when something that resembled a brown human being allegedly flew past them. According to Duncan, the figure glided through the treetops and was in his sight for at least a minute. The other men who were present apparently did not get a look at the entity. This incident took place on November 12, 1966, a good four days before Mothman first made the news.

On November 17, two days after the Scarberry/Mallette incident, a teenage boy from Cheshire, Ohio, claimed that Mothman chased his car along Route 7 in what seems to be a copycat case. He, too, characterized his stalker as being a humanoid monster with amber eyes and ten-foot-long wings.

Four other teenage boys who were exploring the TNT Area on the evening of Saturday, November 20, stated that they came upon the Mothman, and all who were present described it as a gray, man-sized creature with glowing red eyes. Billy Burdette (age 16), Darrell Love (18), Johnny Love (14), and John Morrow (14) were on Camp Conley Road, near Campbell's Creek, when they saw it. To their credit (or perhaps exceedingly poor judgment), the teens attempted to get close to the thing before it flew off. They summarily reported the incident to Deputy Millard Halstead at the local sheriff's office.

Police officers in Charleston, West Virginia, received a call from a gentleman named Richard West around 10:00 the following night, November 21. Mr. West informed them that he had spied a "Batman" perched on the roof of his neighbor's house and had watched the red-eyed being shoot straight up in the air like a helicopter.

Then, some weeks later on Wednesday, January 11, 1967, Linda Scarberry's mother, Mabel McDaniel, was driving on Jackson Avenue, near Tiny's drive-in restaurant on the outskirts of Point Pleasant when she spotted something over Route 62 at around 5:00 p.m. She described it as being brown or dark colored, with an extremely wide wingspan of at least ten feet. Mrs. McDaniel later told John Keel that although she could not see a head or neck, she most definitely thought that the creature had sported humanlike legs. She did not see the thing flap its wings at any time, nor did she hear any audible noises coming from it.

Just an hour and a half earlier on that same day, a man named Chester Leport and a thirteen-year-old named Stevie Pearson Jr. were searching for a Christmas tree in the TNT

Area when a grey thing shot through the air above them at a high rate of speed. Although the object was a good distance away, both witnesses could discern that it was emitting a strange sound. The subject had apparently come from the direction of the Ohio River.

The last notable report of Mothman may have occurred on November 2, 1967, when Mrs. Ralph Thomas (whose property Marcella Bennett was visiting during her encounter) heard a squeaking sound, like a fan belt, outside her home. When she went out to investigate, she claimed she caught a glimpse of something tall and brown moving among the concrete storage igloos in the distance.

Certainly we may never know precisely how many Point Pleasant residents logged sightings of the uncanny creature during that yearlong period. While the accounts listed in this section only represent the ones that obtained a certain level of notoriety by being published in the local paper, other residents may have had Mothman encounters that they kept to themselves for fear of ridicule or of being harassed.

Big Bird Theories

Before the name Mothman was ever even uttered, newspapers in the area were referring to the enigmatic winged creature as the Bird, as residents were grappling to understand precisely what it was that people actually had encountered. By November 18, scores of curiosity seekers had descended on the TNT Area, resulting in lines of cars jam-packing the roadways. Two volunteer firefighters, Captain Paul Yoder and Benjamin Enochs (who were on hand to help control the traffic), alleged that they observed something unusual. "As we were going into the picnic area in the TNT Area, Paul and I saw this white shadow go across the car," Enochs later recalled. "This was about 1:30 a.m. Paul stopped the car and I went into the field, but couldn't see anything. I'd say that this definitely was a large bird of some kind."

An associate professor of wildlife biology from West Virginia University's forestry department soon came forward with his own theory. According to Dr. Robert L. Smith, what people had been seeing was a migratory bird known as a sandhill crane. Standing about five feet tall and with a wingspan up to seven feet across, these impressive birds possess a bright red band across their foreheads that encircles their eyes, but they are apparently not common in West Virginia.

Dr. Smith's theory was reinforced by an incident that took place on November 26, seventy miles north of Point Pleasant in Lowell, Ohio, when a family claimed that they watched four massive gray-and-brown-flecked birds with reddish-colored heads cavorting about in a tree for a considerable amount of time. Over a week later, on December 4, five pilots working at the Gallipolis, Ohio, airport observed an enormous bird that they at first took to be an airplane. It evidently possessed a long neck and was gliding at least seventy miles per hour.

On December 26, 1966, a gentleman named Ace Henry from Gallipolis Ferry shot a white owl with a five-foot-long wingspan that was perched on top of his barn and suggested that perhaps it had been the culprit for all of the Mothman reports.

The bottom line is that although a few of the alleged accounts may have involved misidentifications of large birds, Linda Scarberry and other eyewitnesses were adamant that the thing they had encountered was distinctly humanoid in nature and that there was absolutely no way they could they have merely misidentified something like a large bird.

"Ohio River, Point Pleasant" © Ken Gerhard

The Silver Bridge Disaster

Exactly one year and one month after Mothman burst onto the scene, the Silver Bridge, which spanned the Ohio River joining Point Pleasant with Gallipolis to the west, collapsed, taking forty-six lives. It was December 15, 1967, and the Christmas rush was in full swing. At around 5:00 p.m., as dozens of cars and trucks sat stuck in traffic, the frigid air thundered as one of the suspension chains gave way, felling the structure into the icy waters of the river and taking thirty-one occupied vehicles along with it. Residents were in shock and rushed to the horrific scene in order to search for survivors. The catastrophe still ranks as one of the worst bridge disasters in U.S. history, and it changed the way that older structures are regulated. Aside from the forty-four bodies that were recovered, two victims were never found and nine more people were seriously injured. Everyone knows everyone else in Point Pleasant, and there is no person from that community who did not suffer a terrible loss in the tragedy.

The Silver Bridge had been built in 1928 and had been given its name because it had been coated with silver aluminum paint. Constructed of carbon steel, it was also one of the first high-tension eye-beam bridge designs. Ultimate analysis of the wreckage indicated that there might have been a structural defect involving eye-bar number 330. In addition, the bridge had been subjected to far more traffic and weight than it had ever been designed for, and it had developed a great deal of rust and wear after nearly four decades of brutal, icy winters. Still, there were whispers around Point Pleasant that the catastrophe was somehow linked to Mothman's appearance the year prior. As it turned out, some of the victims had either been Mothman eyewitnesses or relatives of people who had been affected somehow. There was even an unconfirmed rumor that Mothman was spotted near the bridge just before its collapse. Curiously, sightings of the creature diminished abruptly following the Silver Bridge calamity.

The Keelian Legacy

As we can see, during 1967, certain schools of thought had begun to develop with regard to the Mothman. Whether it was the result of mass hysteria or whether an actual monster was frolicking across the Ohio River Valley that year, events seemed to escalate exponentially.

Author John Keel, who penned the definitive book on the subject, *The Mothman Prophecies*, estimated that he had spoken to hundreds of Mothman witnesses during that time, though many of them were too frightened to speak in public. Without question, no one was in a better position to gauge the level of weirdness that was occurring than Keel. A writer and professed UFO enthusiast, he had headed to Point Pleasant in order to get to the bottom of things, acting largely upon the advice of colleague Gray Barker.

Keel quickly formed an alliance with a local reporter named Mary Hyre and set out to gather up all of the information he could. His strange journey is eloquently documented in his excellent book, and anyone looking to peel back more layers of the mystery is encouraged to read it. Rather than rehash a rather complicated chain of events here, I will instead relate my thoughts on how Keel's involvement has colored our perception.

I never had the distinct honor of meeting John Keel, though his work has obviously had a profound impact on me. My adventurous mother first bedazzled me with tales of the West Virginia Mothman when I was a young boy, and it wasn't long before I had my nose firmly planted in Keel's books. His writing style has always struck me as fanciful and also somewhat paranoid. Not that he was not sincere in his convictions. But I've often wondered how well he really did separate the sheep from the goats. So, my eyebrow furled a bit when I read an interview with an oft-quoted eyewitness named Thomas Ury, who admitted that Keel had taken some journalistic license with regard to his sighting.

Ury, a shoe salesman who was on his way to work, claimed that he had spotted a massive bird hovering above his car the morning of November 25, 1966. While he was truly mystified by his sighting, Ury continues to insist that what he saw that day was clearly a gigantic bird and not at all humanoid in nature. Keel had written that Ury's "manlike" creature had taken straight up in the air like a helicopter. Not true, according to Ury. He had first noticed the animal when it soared over some treetops and began circling his convertible hundreds of feet in the air. With an obvious knack for romanticism and a propensity to embellish for the sake of dramatic impact, we must wonder how far Keel took things at times.

It is worth noting that John Keel often referred to himself as a demonologist and that in correspondences with Linda Scarberry and her family, he issued advice on how to deal with evil spirits, as well as where to place crucifixes around their home for protection. It is also generally accepted that he and Mary Hyre spent a great deal of time at the TNT Area together observing amorphous lights in the sky on several occasions. Keel also claimed that he was the victim of intimidation, and he seemed to be concerned that unknown persons were making inquiries about his involvement in the whole affair. His big-picture view was that all of these events were related somehow and that they had global implications. Mothman, UFOs, shadowy visitors, and unseen forces … it was all part of a cosmic puzzle in which Keel placed himself at the nexus.

In my colleague Nick Redfern's book, *The Real Men in Black*, Redfern recounted a story that Keel supposedly told to prolific mystery author Brad Steiger. It involved a visitation from three beings that allegedly entered Keel's Greenwich Village apartment one night by literally materializing through the wall. According to Keel, the Men in Black retrieved a bottle of Clorox from underneath his sink and took sips of it while threatening him. The story is definitely odd, but it is perhaps even stranger that he had never decided to write about the incident. Truth be told, other longtime researchers, friends, and acquaintances of Keel's—including Loren Coleman, Jerome Clark, and Greg Bishop—have all painted him as a bit of a trickster and a storyteller. My point is that I know many investigators who view Keel as an infallible character and have accepted all of his musings as the gospel truth. There's no doubt that he was onto something, but was it really the cosmic conspiracy that he made it out to be?

Conspiracies and Curses

Ultimately, with regard to the Mothman riddle, we are still left with many questions and no real answers. John Keel seemed to believe that there was an extraterrestrial involvement of some sort. Not the typical little gray men from another planet per se but some complex mechanism that was working from an alternate plane of interdimensional origin. From his perspective, this shadowy intelligence was focused intently on the region surrounding Point Pleasant during that time period, and the UFO and MIB appearances were evidence of that. It is true that in the months after Mothman's arrival, the headlines in the local papers reported numerous sightings of unidentified luminous objects in the sky, which were observed by many townsfolk. Perhaps drinking Keel's Kool-Aid, witness Linda Scarberry felt that both Mothman and the UFOs were merely distractions so that no one would notice the Men in Black who were tooling around town in black cadillacs, following some incomprehensible agenda, no doubt.

John Keel's overlying theory is quite intriguing. If there really is some omnipotent force capable of manifesting and interacting with us in various forms, then it has been around since time began. It could in fact explain (in one fell swoop) every unexplained phenomenon from monsters to ghosts, faeries, miracles, UFOs, and the like. While I embrace the concept to some extent, I am hesitant to do so wholeheartedly, as there is an anthropomorphic element that implies we humans are important enough to be bothered with in the first place, which I am reluctant to accept. However, admittedly I have not been immersed in the subject matter to the extent of someone like Andy Colvin.

Colvin, who has written three books in a series titled The Mothman's Photographer (in addition to two other related works), grew up about forty-five miles from Point Pleasant. At an early age, one of Colvin's childhood friends claimed that he had had a vision of the Mothman in relation to an impending disaster. The two boys literally built a shrine to the creature, which they viewed as some kind of superhero. Later, Colvin took an unrelated photo that seemed to show the apparition's face peering in a window of his house. Ultimately, many other strange coincidences began to emerge, and events began to affect his life in a dramatic way.

Colvin has been obsessively immersed in research for the better part of his life and seems to accept the multifaceted doctrine advocated by Keel, as well as writer Gray Barker. Moreover, he senses that Mothman has a very strong link to other mysteries, including precognition, extraterrestrials, and the occult. Like Keel, he thinks that the CIA, military, and other government agencies have been keenly aware of these occurrences for years and have conspired to keep them from us.

But Colvin doesn't necessarily view Mothman as being malevolent. In a recent phone conversation, he told me that, similar to the Garuda of Hindu culture, the entity's manifestation represents a metamorphosis in our lives, a hallucination metaphorically stemming from the cocoon of our unconscious minds. In this sense, Mothman is a guardian of sorts.

My colleague Nick Redfern, who spent a week with Colvin back in 2010, told me he feels that Colvin's work is important because rather than simply revisiting historical accounts, he has ferreted out many modern sightings and views these encounters as part of an alternative paradigm of high strangeness … a cosmic spectrum that radiates outward, appearing when we least expect it. Case in point, while Redfern and Colvin were visiting a UFO Mecca known as Giant Rock in the California desert, they stumbled upon a great face that had been painted on a rock wall. The face looked remarkably similar to eyewitness sketches of England's Owlman. Within a short time span, other Owlman-related incidents were perceived by Redfern, Colvin, and other Fortean researchers they knew.

On a more ominous note, a well-known paranormal investigator and former law enforcement officer named Rick Moran promoted the idea that the Mothman phenomenon was the result of a U.S. military–sponsored mind-control experiment and that the people of Point Pleasant acted as guinea pigs, so to speak. It would not be the first time that covert operations intended to cause sociological breakdown have been employed by the military. In a bizarre and tragic twist of fate, Moran died mysteriously and unexpectedly at a reasonably young age, adding more fuel to the conspiracy theory. Before his death, he stated that his family had been the victims of intimidating phone calls and threats.

There are also those who point to the toxic environment of the TNT Area and wonder if Mothman might be some type of mutation, spawned by the mixture of lethal chemicals that are infused into the environment there. Following World War II, several of the concrete storage igloos were leased out to various chemical companies, who used them to store, among other things, cyanide. Tests conducted in the McClintic Wildlife Management Area by environmental scientists during 1981 confirmed that the entire water supply was extremely hazardous due to pollution from the previous tenants. In May of 2010, one of the igloos that still contained twenty thousand pounds of hazardous materials exploded, leading to the reserve being closed to the public until further notice. The spot remains on the Environmental Protection Agency's National Priority List. If there is any place capable of perpetuating a sci-fi scenario where owls mutate into giant, manlike monsters, I suppose this would be it.

Then there's the matter of two curses; or a curse within a curse, depending on how you look at it. The first involves a proud Shawnee warrior named Hokoleskwa, which translates roughly to "cornstalk." The region around Point Pleasant was at one time embroiled in a bitter war between the Native American people and a British army that was embarking on a bloodthirsty land grab. Following a savage battle in 1774, Chief Cornstalk and his forces were betrayed and defeated by the opposition, and he was ultimately executed. It is widely believed that his last words invoked a mighty curse on the area that would span two hundred years. Many of the locals secretly blame the curse for the Silver Bridge disaster, in addition to a general decline in the local economy. Consequently, there are those who consider Mothman's reign during the 1960s to be somehow related to Chief Cornstalk's curse.

The other imprecation involves Mothman directly. Author Loren Coleman has been the primary chronicler of some eighty instances where individuals who bore strong connections to the mystery met an untimely or unusually swift demise. We have already mentioned the late Rick Moran, but there are apparently many others ranging from relatives of various eyewitnesses to reporter Mary Hyre and even book publishers and television producers that had been the principals in Mothman-related media projects.

My friend Jon Downes, a leading British cryptozoologist and author, experienced an episode of "psychic backlash" at a time when he was writing a book about the flying humanoid dubbed the Owlman; other researchers have also mentioned negative fallout while investigating these types of cases.

Whether we choose to believe it or not, there appear to be adverse repercussions for those who decide to involve themselves in these matters.

"Owlman Face on Giant Rock" © Nick Redfern

A Recent Sighting

Following my appearance on a nationally syndicated radio show, I was contacted by a man named John Hipes, who wanted to relate his own personal encounter to me. John grew up in the Point Pleasant area during the 1970s after his family had moved there from Detroit. As a boy, he had heard rumors about the Mothman and had played at the fairgrounds adjacent to the McClintic Wildlife Management Area, where his father had also hunted. John remembers Linda Scarberry as "a very normal person who didn't seek any attention." He had worked with her younger sister and had also attended school with Marcella Bennett's son. John recalls that residents at that time seemed more concerned about the identity of the Men in Black that had come to town as opposed to the identity of the Mothman creature.

In John's own words:

This past winter, my wife and I were driving from Huntington to Point Pleasant at about 11:00 p.m. Route 2 is deer infested, so driving becomes a hyper-alert situation as we scan for deer. As we were coming close to the historic Jenkins house and the "wetlands," we both saw something on the right side of the road on a bridge. We know the bridge runs over a railroad and there is a big drop-off, so at about three hundred yards, I slowed way down so the "deer" could come off the bridge and not spook it to its death. Then, the figure stood up and what looked like a wing unfurled, and off the bridge it went. The angle of the body and moonlight/headlight showed the body from the back, and we could see the left wing. The body was flush with the retaining wall of the bridge, and the tip extended into the lane over the white line—twelve to sixteen feet. The body was well over five feet. My wife and I are both nurses, psych nurses at that, so we are great at quick observation and assessment. My wife screeched a bit…out of character. No way was this an owl, as the body was way too big. Very odd.

During a thorough phone interview, John struck me as an extremely credible witness who simply observed an unusually large, winged animal that he couldn't identify. Having regularly seen cranes and other large birds over the years, he was sure that whatever the thing was, it was just way too massive to be easily explained. Perhaps the Mothman, whatever its identity may be, still lingers in the area to this day.

"Mothman Statue" © Ken Gerhard

My Own Investigation

"Where are you headed?" I had barely heard the man sitting next to me because I was staring out the tiny portal window, gazing down at the clouds. I was totally transfixed by the sound of the jet's droning engines.

"Point Pleasant," I finally muttered.

"No kidding," the man replied, "that's where I grew up." At this point I was taken aback. It was the latest in a series of strange incidents that had coincided with my preparations over the course of the previous week. "Point Pleasant is famous because of the Mothman," the man continued. He was a pleasant-looking, sandy-blond-haired man in his late thirties dressed in casual business attire.

A wide grin spread across my face as I responded, "That's actually why I'm heading there. I'm going to do an investigation for a television show."

Once again, his reply was utterly unexpected: "Really? I actually lost one of my closest childhood friends in the Silver Bridge collapse."

Being that Point Pleasant boasts a population of less than 5,000 in a state of almost two million people, I thought it odd that one of its sons sat next to me on this very plane, despite the fact that I was flying to Charleston, West Virginia, at the time. I tried to calculate the odds in my head, but math was never my strong point. The coincidence was made even stranger by the fact that the day before, I had met two women from Point Pleasant at a conference in Texas, over 1,000 miles away. And just days earlier, I had experienced one of the most unnerving experiences of my life when a pane of glass shattered right before my very eyes as I spoke to a co-worker at her place of business. There was no reason for it to have occurred. Nothing was near the glass at the

time. Most disconcerting was the fact that the glass had remained in its frame, albeit fragmented, and at the top of the break—two discernible, round impressions that reminded me of large eyes. Such is the world of Mothman.

As I drove from Charleston to Point Pleasant, I couldn't help but notice that the roads meandered through rolling hills and pastures that were surrounded by murky forests and dotted with rustic farmhouses. It struck me as the ideal landscape for a Hollywood slasher movie.

Upon arriving in town, I checked in at the historic Lowe Hotel. The older gentleman at the front desk inquired whether I was part of the television crew that was in town filming. "I don't care much for that skeptic they brought in here," he confided in me. "Comes off as very condescending. Folks around here know what they saw."

After unpacking my bags, I strolled over to the Mothman Museum. Established by local researcher Jeff Wamsley, the museum hosts an impressive array of original newspaper clippings and artifacts, including a life-sized model of Mothman at the entrance. Guests are encouraged to take advantage of the wide selection of souvenirs for sale—T-shirts, bumper stickers, and the like. I asked the cashier if Wamsley was around, and he mumbled something about the owner being more elusive than Mothman himself.

While I was perusing the exhibit, iconic author and crypto-zoologist Loren Coleman wandered in. Loren had been brought in to act as official historian for the TV production, while my role was to mount an on-site investigation and comment on the supernatural elements of the case. As a longtime researcher, Loren has written about the Mothman phenomenon for years. Although he has at times taken a somewhat Fortean approach to the subject in his work, he also endorses the theory that the creature may in fact be some type of unknown, man-sized owl or gigantic bird. He and I exchanged pleasantries for a few minutes and then posed for some photos with a family of tourists who had recognized the two of us. Since I had a couple of hours before my interview, I decided to grab a burger at the local café, which was reminiscent of an authentic 1950s diner. I was tempted to ask some of the other customers about the Mothman but got the sense that residents had tired of the subject.

Following a fine meal, I went down to the Ohio River to view the Silver Bridge Memorial and to pay my respects. The remembrance is located where the structure had once stood. One cannot help but feel humbled and sad whilst reading the list of victims. It certainly put things into perspective for me. I spent a few more minutes wandering the seemingly deserted Main Street of the town. There was a certain indefinable electricity in the air. Whether it could be traced to the fact that I was aware of the utterly strange events that had transpired there decades earlier, I cannot say.

At one point, a homeless man with a scraggly beard and dressed in camouflage fatigues wandered by me as he rambled something to himself. This struck me as unusual, as he seemed to be the only person I saw that was out and about.

The final stop on my mini-tour was the silver life-sized statue of Mothman in the town's square. Admittedly stylized, it stands as a monument to Point Pleasant's weird legacy. Across the street from the statue, I noticed a quaint gift shop with Mothman memorabilia for sale. When I entered the establishment, I recognized the shop's proprietor as Bob Lander. A former truck driver who has lived a colorful and adventurous life, Bob showed me some photos that he had taken inside some of TNT Area's concrete bunkers. They seemed to show spherical orbs of light dancing in front of the camera. An enlargement of one of the orbs displayed an image that Bob insisted was the face of Mothman. Drawing from his Native American heritage, he explained to me how the being was a spiritual entity that his people had known about for centuries.

I subsequently met up with the film crew back at the museum. The segment was being produced for a Canadian television program called *Weird or What?* and would be hosted by actor William Shatner, star of the immensely popular science fiction series *Star Trek*. Unfortunately, I learned that Shatner's scenes would be filmed in California, so I would not have the great honor of meeting him.

After an interview in which I expressed various opinions about the monstrous nature of Mothman, the crew drove me out to a wooded area north of town. We had learned that the TNT Area and surrounding McClintic Wildlife Management Area were currently off-limits and surrounded by a tall fence because of an explosion two years prior, so we concentrated on a wooded tract nearby. I set about putting up some motion-activated cameras and broadcasting distressed animal calls from a speaker system. My reasoning was that if Mothman were a gigantic owl, as some have suggested, the calls would draw it in where I could capture its image. But because we were on a tight schedule, the experiment was too brief to yield any results.

I left Point Pleasant tantalized but certainly no closer to finding any definitive answers than John Keel or scores of other researchers that came before me. The only conclusion I could reach was that the community of Point Pleasant had in fact been the epicenter of a remarkable visitation all those years ago. For whatever reason, an unearthly winged entity had paid a visit during the winter of 1966, leaving an indelible mark on many. But the story doesn't end there.

SIX

Mexico: The Sky
Gods Return

The nation of Mexico is a vast and mysterious place. With a land surface area that spans over 760,000 square miles and a population of about 112 million people, the country possesses lengthy coasts on two different oceans and displays a wide diversity of climates, habitats, and cultures. In addition, Mexico boasts a long and intriguing history that dates back thousands years and includes several notable and surprisingly advanced civilizations, including the Olmec, Toltec, Zapotec, Teotihuacan, Maya, and Aztec. All of these early empires demonstrated remarkable capacities with regard to writing, mathematics, art, architecture, and astronomy. The similarities to comparable civilizations that had once flourished in the Middle East are striking. Of prime example is the presence of massively impressive pyramids that once paid homage to a variety of kings and deities, many of whom were believed to have dwelt in the heavens.

Fast-forward to modern times. On the afternoon of July 11, 1991, countless citizens had gathered in the streets of Mexico City in order to witness a rare total solar eclipse. As the crowds stared in wonderment up at the darkened sky, thousands of people began to observe (and in several cases film) something else that was quite unexpected...a shiny, oblate object that appeared much too large and far too close to merely be a distant star or planet. Subsequent analysis of several corroborating videotapes seemed to confirm that the UFO was silver, disc-like, and that it cast a dark shadow on its underside. Mexican flying saucer reports were certainly nothing new, but this particular event seemed to usher in an intense new wave of UFO activity over that particular nation.

Because the old culture of Mexico remains steeped in superstition and mysticism, often exhibiting a flair for romanticism, major news networks around the nation began to broadcast the reports in dramatic fashion. A multitude of UFO research groups quickly sprang up, intent on documenting the intense phenomenon that was now permeating their homeland.

Hombrecito Volador

One of Mexico's most respected UFO researchers is Santiago Yturria. I had the great honor and pleasure of meeting and visiting with Yturria at his home in Monterrey, Mexico, in 2009. His large collection of UFO videos, reports, and archives is impressive, as is his collection of musical instruments. You see, Yturria also happens to be a Grammy-nominated musician who brings that same passion and professionalism to his research into anomalous flying objects. From his high rooftop, he constantly scours the sky over Monterrey on a nightly basis, hoping to catch a glimpse of something inexplicable. Of extreme interest are his investigations into subjects that he refers to as UFHs—Unidentified Flying Humanoids, or, in his native Spanish tongue, the *Hombrecito Volador*, or "Little Flying Man."

In an article published in 2005, Yturria chronicled several videos that have been made public in recent years, which seem to show humanoid-shaped figures hovering high in the stratosphere over Mexico. The original clips were captured by a handful of respected UFO "sky watchers" who have spent a considerable amount of time scanning the skies for enigmatic objects. It appears that a researcher named Amado Marquez was the first person to observe and film one of these UFHs. Amado's home city of Cuernavaca in the state of Morelos lies just south of Mexico City, and it was here that the investigator was staked out on his rooftop one day in February of 2000. As he aimed his camera up into the sky, Amado observed what he at first took to be an unidentified object coming into view. But as he zoomed in on the subject, the UFO clearly resembled a man in an upright position with two recognizable legs dangling down. Amado was able to discern that there was no parachute, hang glider, or other apparatus keeping the "man" airborne, nor did he hear any engine noise or observe any emission that would indicate a jet pack was in use. The figure was dark but was too tiny for Amado to make out any other details, other than the fact that he was soaring horizontally at a slow speed. Unsure of precisely what it was that he had captured on film, Amado decided to keep the video to himself at first.

The very next month, a colleague of Amado's named Salvador Guerrero had a remarkably similar experience in the nearby city of Colonia Agricola Oriental. The being that Guerrero videotaped also resembled a man with two visible legs hovering in the air. Its arms were outstretched and its posture was upright, though it was leaning forward slightly. The entity appeared to be wearing a garment like a hoodie with material draping below its arms. While Guerrero filmed, the UFH drifted out of sight behind a building. Guerrero made the bold decision to go public with his video, and it was subsequently posted on some Internet websites. Meanwhile, back in Cuernavaca, UFO hunter Gerardo Valenzuela captured another flying humanoid on film in July of 2000, though this one appeared tall and lanky with a slender body. The figure had descended cautiously through a valley and had vanished behind a rise while Gerardo filmed. A curious pattern was developing.

Newspapers began to pick up on the story by October, when *La Prensa* ran an article about a sighting that was logged by a professional airline pilot. According to the clipping, "A commercial airplane pilot from AeroCalifornia who wanted to hide his name in order to avoid problems at work, reported the sighting of a 'little flying man' who was flying at the same altitude as the plane before landing. According to the pilot this 'hombrecito volador' had a kind of backpack and was flying freely. The pilot added that he, 'clearly saw its arms and legs.'"

Other UFHs would be documented in the skies over Mexico during the following decade. A woman named Ana Luisa Cid captured an incident on video that Santiago Yturria refers to as the "Entity Reunion in the Sky." On February 14, 2004, Ana Luisa, along with two other observers, filmed three dark shapes high up in the sky over Mexico City. Though they were a great distance away, the objects appeared to interact with each other in unusual ways. For example, at one point a diminutive figure that was situated below the primary target ascended rapidly and was literally absorbed by the thing, which seemed to possess either winglike appendages or perhaps propellers. Within moments, an even smaller object broke free and flew quickly away from the others. Though the resulting footage is rather ambiguous because of the extreme distance, one of the more pronounced figures in the video jerks around in a rather erratic manner and somewhat resembles a person wearing a flowing cape.

A student named Horacio Roquet Lopez was the next person to document an encounter. As he exited his apartment building on the morning of June 17, 2005, Horacio spotted a manlike being hovering over his neighborhood in Mexico City. The entity appeared to remain aloft with the aid of a contraption that emitted or reflected a glowing reddish light. Horacio was so amazed that he sprinted back up to his apartment and alerted his sister while simultaneously grabbing a video camera that they owned. The figure was still visible when he and his sister returned to the spot on the street where Horacio had been standing, and they were able to film the UFH as it floated overhead. Despite the shakiness of the handheld shot, once Horacio had zoomed in tightly on the aerial subject, the resulting footage turned out to be some of the most detailed to date and seemed to show a dark humanoid in some kind of spacesuit with massively square shoulders, straddling a platformlike contrivance.

Some fairly recent videos include a widely disseminated piece of footage that was captured on May 17, 2006, by a group of UFO researchers affiliated with Ovni Club Nuevo León. At the time, the investigators were staked out in the mountains north of Monterrey's Cerro de las Mitras when they observed and filmed what appeared to be a hooded, cloaked being stepping off of a mountain peak and then gliding through the air in an even trajectory for several minutes.

Enlargements of the film revealed that the figure seemed to be holding something in its arms, perhaps a small animal. Witnesses stated that there was an eerie silence in the area at the time. The clip created quite a buzz on the Internet, but subsequent analysis by experts seemed to suggest that the object might have been affixed to a cable or wire, as if it were somehow suspended in the air. Debate about this particular video continues.

On February 28, 2008, a man named Daniel Sanchez captured the image of a flying humanoid entity that was seen by both him and his nephew near the Mexico City Airport. They both described the being as resembling an astronaut in a spacesuit, and it appeared as though the figure was looking around and surveying his surroundings. Though there appear to be many of these UFH videotapes in existence, they are so utterly controversial that experts can't seem to agree on precisely what it is that they show. One possibility that has been suggested is that the objects are actually man-shaped balloons or balloon clusters that are being launched into the air on purpose, a theory that we cannot discount in some of the cases.

"Leonardo Samaniego" © Ken Gerhard

Flying Witch Attacks
Monterrey Police Officer

In May of 2009, I hopped a short flight from my home in San Antonio, Texas, to the industrial Mexican city of Monterrey. I had been hired by the producers of the television show *MonsterQuest* to conduct an investigation into the flying humanoid reports for a new episode they were filming at the time. As the jetliner made its descent, I took note of Monterrey's apparent isolation. It reminded me of an urban oasis, nestled in a round valley like a great bowl, with craggy, ancient mountains and desert wilderness encircling its outer limits. I'd traveled to Mexico about half a dozen times in my lifetime but had never before visited the northern interior.

Upon entering the airport, we were met by an ominous sight, seemingly right out of a Michael Crichton novel, as customs officials with surgical masks and latex gloves were examining people for signs of the H1N1 virus that was spreading throughout the country at that time. It was obvious that the government was attempting to enact a sort of quarantine in order to keep the pandemic in check. Looking back now, I can't help but wonder if there was some significance to the timing of the outbreak and recent sightings of a Mothman type of creature in Mexico around that same time period.

I quickly cleared customs and made my way to the taxi stand, but because I don't speak Spanish, I simply handed the driver a copy of a local newspaper clipping I had brought with me. The article's headline boldly stated, "*Causa 'bruja' desmayo a policía de Guadalupe.*" My chauffeur nodded and smiled, and we were on our way.

As we drove south through Monterrey, I made note of the rustic, old-world surroundings and colorful buildings that adorned the city. Finally we arrived at our destination, the Guadalupe Police Station on the southeast edge of town. Exiting the cab, I climbed the steps, entered the brick building, and presented my handy and helpful newspaper clipping to the female receptionist at the front desk. The woman nodded at me politely and led me through the station hallways until we had reached a closed door in an official-looking area. We could hear murmured voices emanating from inside the room. I knocked lightly on the door and opened it slowly.

I instantly recognized the man being interviewed as Officer Leonardo Samaniego. His image adorned the newspaper clipping that I had been carrying along with me, and I had seen his youthful face before on Mexican news broadcasts. Seated across from Leonardo was a three-man film crew, as well as UFO researcher Santiago Yturria. I quietly took a seat in the back and listened intently as the discussion continued.

Yturria posed his questions to the young officer in Spanish and then graciously translated the answers back to English for my benefit, as well as that of the Canadian production team. I was by now well familiar with the incident in question, but hearing Leonardo tell the story firsthand was riveting, to say the least.

At several junctures he began to become emotional and tear up as he relived that terrifying evening that had changed his life forever. Leonardo confessed to us that he still had vivid nightmares about the encounter and occasionally woke up in a panic with sweat streaming down his face. I wondered if the fact that I was dressed all in black with my trademark black leather cowboy hat (adorned with a silver skull, no less) made him slightly uncomfortable.

His story began at about 3:15 the morning of January 16, 2004. Leonardo was alone on patrol, cruising the neighborhood streets of Guadalupe. There had been word of a burglary suspect on the loose in the area. As he slowly turned onto Alamo Street, he suddenly noticed a black object floating down from a large tree just in front of him. At first, Leonardo thought the thing resembled a large plastic garbage bag, but when he hit the brakes, he was able to make out more details in his headlights. He couldn't believe what he was seeing.

The object appeared to be a woman wearing a dark, hooded cloak. Her skin was dark brown, and her eyes were enormous, black, and completely lidless. The entity hovered seamlessly a few feet off of the ground for a moment before landing feet first in front of Leonardo's patrol car. According to the officer, she was none too pleased with the intense light that was being emitted from his high beams and in fact raised her hand up in front of her face to shield her eyes, turning her head away briefly.

Completely unsure about what he was up against, Leonardo threw his car into reverse and began to call for backup on his radio. At the end of the block, he turned his face back forward and that's when the hag appeared at lightening speed, pouncing on the hood of his vehicle and clawing at him through the windshield in a frantic fashion. This was evidently too much for poor Leonardo to bear, as he lost consciousness. Several minutes later, the stunned policeman was revived by responding officers, though his attacker was nowhere to be found. An ambulance was called to the scene, since Leonardo was visibly in a state of shock.

Some local televisions news reporters showed up to interview him. A description of the *bruja* (witch) was broadcasted, around Mexico the next evening, and the world took notice of the unbelievable story. Subsequently, Leonardo was taken to a local hospital and tested for drugs, alcohol, stress, or any psychological condition that may have caused him to have a hallucination. The results came back negative.

We might be inclined to dismiss Leonardo's encounter as a complete aberration if not for the fact that others soon came forward claiming that they, too, had seen the flying witch on prior occasions—including some other officers from his precinct, as well as residents from the community of Guadalupe. One person even produced a video purporting to show the cloaked figure soaring high over the neighborhood.

"La Huasteca" © Ken Gerhard

An Investigation

Following Leonardo's interview, he was gracious enough to provide the producers of *MonsterQuest* with a re-creation of the actual incident. We all piled into a van and rode over to the exact location on Alamo Street where he had encountered the entity some five years earlier. There was nothing particularly unusual about the spot that I could discern. Just an ordinary neighborhood lane with several modest residences interspersed with a few industrial warehouses. The landmark of Cerra de la Silla Mountain loomed high in the background.

A multitude of neighborhood children filtered out into the street in order to watch the film crew at work, and I wondered how they felt about the possibility of a flying witch taking up residence in their neighborhood. Did they view the entire affair as merely a tall tale, or lock their doors at night, afraid to venture out into the darkness?

Leonardo climbed into a patrol car on loan from his police department and reenacted the entire incident. In absentia of a stand-in witch, it was explained that Computer Generated Imagery (CGI) special effects would be applied in post-production editing to make it all work.

The very next morning, I met up with local UFO researcher Marco Reynoso. Marco is the former head of the regional chapter of the Mutual UFO Network. Over breakfast, he told me about a remarkable experience that had set him on a lifelong quest for real answers. Apparently, when he was a young boy growing up in Monterrey, Marco had observed a tiny, winged, humanoidlike creature peeking out from behind his kitchen curtains one evening. The diminutive being reminded him of a gargoyle, with long, black hair covering its body and batlike wings (see *Ikals* in the Appendix). To his credit, Marco made an attempt to curtail the goblin, but the entity vanished right before his very eyes.

Next, we both met up with the film crew and headed out to an extremely remote and mysterious valley in the nearby Sierra Madre Mountains known as La Huasteca. Once there we were joined by a local climbing guide named Sergio Estavillo, who had agreed to lead us on an exploration of the local cave systems. It stood to reason that if there were elusive batlike humanoids in the area, they might seek refuge in these cavernous hideaways. Needless to say, we ultimately did not locate our quarry during filming, though the opportunity to explore a huge cavern at an altitude of 5,000 feet was an adventure, to say the least. Though, I did have an unfortunate and painful run-in with a thorny weed that Sergio referred to as a "bitch plant."

On the way back to Monterrey, we stopped to interview a local rancher named Simon Laero Orrela, who described some UFOs the locals had been seeing in the skies overhead as of late. Although he was not familiar with flying humanoids specifically, I did hear Simon reference the infamous Latino monster known as the Chupacabra.

Before leaving La Huasteca, I observed some 3,000-year-old prehistoric stone carvings that had presumably been made by the earliest people to settle in the area. Some of the images seemed to represent disc-shaped objects hovering in the sky.

Wrapping up our investigation, we made one last stop at the home of Santiago Yturria in order to view his extensive collection of videos clips that purported to show the enigmatic flying humanoids of Mexico. Admittedly, I left Monterrey as befuddled as ever. The only conclusion I could reach was that a diverse collection of airborne weirdos were making their presence known throughout the expansive nation … and evidently they have been there for a very long time.

Cave at La Huasteca © Ken Gerhard

Mexican Mothman

Shortly before I traveled to Monterrey in 2009, a university student from La Junta, Guerrero, Mexico, claimed that he had a terrifying encounter with a winged humanoid while driving home from school on the evening of Friday, March 6. Traveling on a remote thoroughfare, the young man had noticed something hunched down on the side of the road ahead of him that resembled a man huddled beneath a blanket.

When he tapped on his brakes to take a look, the figure rose up, took two leaps forward, and unfurled enormous batlike wings, taking flight. The monster allegedly chased the student for about fifteen minutes, peering into the passenger window of his speeding car. The student's description of the entity was quite chilling—about six feet tall and manlike with red, bloodshot eyes, two sets of wings (larger in front, smaller in back), and diminutive, kangaroo-like arms that it held loosely, as if they were lacking in strength and substance. Its entire face appeared to be covered in fur, and its forehead was dome shaped.

UFH over Santa Monica, California

While primarily a Mexican phenomenon, there are some indications that UFHs are occasionally seen hovering over other parts of North America and the world. According to Ed Sherwood, a British UFO and crop circle researcher living in California, he and his wife, Kris, observed and filmed a humanoid-shaped figure over their Santa Monica neighborhood on November 27, 2004. The couple was out walking their dog around 10:15 a.m. when Ed noticed an object high up in the sky that he could not easily identify. At first, he pondered the possibility that the thing might be a helicopter, based on its altitude, speed, and trajectory. Yet it seemed substantially smaller and was not making any sound. As he strained his eyes, Ed began to feel that the object had a distinctly humanoid shape. He immediately recalled a presentation by Santiago Yturria that he had attended three months earlier in which Yturria had made a strong case for the UFH phenomenon.

Fearing he might miss an opportunity to document his very own sighting, Ed ran back to his home to retrieve a video camera while Kris remained focused on the anomaly in order to keep track of its position. For the next fifteen minutes or so, Ed attempted to capture the figure on film, though its great distance (Ed estimates that it was at least 700 feet up in the air) and the fact that it was moving away from his position made it very difficult to keep it in frame, particularly as he attempted to zoom in on it. The resulting video clips only span a few minutes total. But they do seem to verify a familiar motif. The object appeared to resemble a bulky, human shape with outstretched arms, though it actually possessed a total of six appendages. Ed estimated that the thing stood seven to eight feet tall.

As a result of an article about the incident that he posted on his website, Ed received a corroborating letter in March of 2007 that stated:

> I have a friend who will remain unnamed that is a service man on Edwards Air Force Base, who encountered what he and his partner recognized to be a human-shaped silhouette floating above the local church; while driving towards the church they both looked at it in awe, attempting to figure out what they both concurred to be seeing. Once

verbally mentioning it, the UFH began to approach their vehicle, and followed them to their work quarters. Ten feet in front of their vehicle, and approximately 40 feet above, with precision trailing, whatever it was IT WAS FOLLOWING HIS VEHICLE. Being seen more times throughout the day, two other members saw the UFH, and later wrote my friend an e-mail stating: "I hope you guys aren't playing any pranks because I just saw what you guys were talking about, and it wasn't a pleasant encounter. I goggled [sic] flying shadows and came to a video of the Mexican Flying Humanoids, which resembled what we all saw on the base."

This is not a joke, my friend is within blocks' distance of where this occurred on base, and was frightful. His words when he encountered this sighting. "I thought this was something evil, it looked like the grim reaper. It was so close and so clear but we starred [sic] in astonishment trying to comply what we were looking at. It looked like a dark-clothed person, just floating above the church.... It was surreal." After explaining to me what happened he mentioned that the hairs on his arms were standing up, and he didn't think he could sleep tonight.

The letter writer summarized by explaining that his soldier friend feared any potential repercussions for going public with his sighting and therefore had decided to remain anonymous.

The Flying Man
of Cannock Chase

Cannock Chase, Staffordshire, in central England is a sizeable wooded area where one can observe and enjoy a diversity of plant and animal life. A multitude of tourists and hikers frequent the region on a regular basis. But since the nineteenth century, Cannock Chase has also gained a widespread reputation as a place of high weirdness and mystery. Accounts of ghosts and strange creatures—including so-called Devil Dogs and Black Panthers, werewolves, and Bigfoot beings—surface from time to time, and there are also many who claimed to have seen UFOs in the skies above the serene forests. Within the past few years, there has apparently been at least one report of a flying humanoid as well. According to Fortean investigator Nick Redfern, the incident was published in a local newspaper. Redfern tells the strange story in his book, *Mystery Animals of the British Isles: Staffordshire*:

> What was without any doubt the strangest of all stories of unidentified flying entities seen in the skies of Staffordshire surfaced on February 19, 2009, when *Chase Post* editor Mike Lockley stated that nothing less than a flying man had been seen soaring over and around Cannock Chase! Five locals have contacted the Post after witnessing the figure traveling, seemingly unaided, over houses at around 11 am on Sunday, February 8. One described it as a "Superman" moment … Lockley added: "But eagle-eyed Boney Hay villager Clive Wright believes those who

reckon they witnessed something supernatural are talking a load of kryptonite." The 68-year-old, who spotted the flying man from the living room window of his Sunnymead Road home, believes the pilot was traveling with the aid of a jet pack—a strap-on engine made famous in the 1965 James Bond movie, *Thunderball.* Clive's wife, Janet, 68, and 14-year-old grandson Nicholas also witnessed the Chase's own rocket man. Clive said: "To say it was strange would be an understatement. And the 'bottle' didn't come into it because none of us drink. At first I was watching quite a number of seagulls and noticed what I thought was one in the middle moving quite slowly. I got up to take a close look and realized it was a flying man. I searched the sky for the plane he had bailed out of, but could see nothing."

The *Post* additionally quoted Clive Wright as saying, "All I could see was this man traveling in a controlled, straight line, traveling from Ryecroft shops across to Gentleshaw Common. I immediately went upstairs to get my binoculars and went out in the backyard, but he was gone. Some kind of Dan Dare spacemen—that's what it looked like. The only explanation is that he was wearing a jet pack, although I was surprised he was traveling over a densely populated area."

Redfern concludes, "Whether an intrepid flyer equipped with a startlingly high-tech piece of aerial gadgetry or not, the mystery of Staffordshire's flying man remains."

Reports from Poland

There are two flying humanoid accounts from the nation of Poland that seem to fit nicely into this particular chapter in terms of the general time frame and flavor. The first incident was observed by a young hospital medic named Mariusz as he was cycling with a friend between Koniewo and Lidzbark during the autumn of 2000. The eyewitness decided to share his experience with a noted Polish UFO researcher in 2007.

According to Mariusz, as the two men pedaled slowly past a small forested area on a bright, moonlit night, they both heard a loud, rumbling noise like a heavy metal band reverberating from the trees. Just then, the cyclists noticed the figure of a gray-colored, long-haired man flying along on his side, while facing them. Mariusz's companion apparently lost it at this point, throwing his bike to the ground and running away in a state of panic "as every normal man in a similar situation" would do. The sighting only lasted a few seconds, since the levitating being disappeared quickly into the trees. But Mariusz remained there in a trance, listening to the strange and terrifying noise that would seemingly fade away and then get louder. Ultimately, he chose to follow his friend's lead and retreated in the same direction that he had fled minutes earlier.

When the two men had reunited down the road, both of them were literally trembling and in tears. To this day, Mariusz regards the entire affair with an uneasy feeling, admitting that he had never believed in ghosts or the unexplained up to that point.

In another Polish case, researcher Lon Strickler, administrator of the Phantoms and Monsters website, received a bulletin from a woman identified as Mrs. Izydora. She evidently was on holiday in the Borne Sulinowo region in 2008 when she claimed that she had an encounter with a semitransparent airborne humanoid. While her husband explored the nearby woods on that particular day, Mrs. Izydora chose to take a leisurely walk around a deserted military base. That's when she began to feel uncomfortable before observing a "misty" entity hovering above her a good distance off the ground. Her impression was that the figure resembled a tall man with a discernible white outline. The apparition seemed to be holding its arms in an outstretched position. Similar to other eyewitnesses, she was paralyzed with fear and felt completely disoriented. When Mrs. Izydora began to head back to her vehicle, she was horrified to realize that the being was following her, though ultimately it took off up into the air and vanished from her sight. The seventy-one-year-old woman pleaded with her husband to drive her home immediately but didn't reveal her reasons to him until two days had passed.

As we can see, the new millennium has ushered in a whole new age of flying humanoids that, for the most part, are lacking the wings and animal-like characteristics of their predecessors. These so-called aeronauts (or whatever they are) appear to possess supernatural abilities and a covert agenda that involves frightening the living daylights out of anyone that is unfortunate enough to cross their path.

SEVEN

Recent Reports

As we plod onward into the twenty-first century, it seems like it should be easy for us to distance ourselves from these ostensibly mythological beings, except for one disturbing fact. They are not obliging us by merely fading into the past. In fact, I continue to gather relevant reports from seemingly credible people whose encounters with the flying humanoids have affected them in very profound ways. It would appear that whatever mechanism has spawned these uncanny airborne visitors for the last five millennia remains with us even still. In the following pages are some examples of flying humanoid accounts that have surfaced in recent years, many of which I have had an opportunity to investigate personally.

The descriptions have remained intriguingly consistent with those that have been documented by previous investigators over the course of decades.

"Humanoid Sketch" © Frank Ramirez

San Antonio Artist Sees and Sketches Bizarre Being

A profoundly chilling encounter from the late 1990s that didn't come to light until 2007 involves a man named Frank Ramirez. Having gotten to know Frank on a personal basis, I find him to be an impressively credible eyewitness and steadfast in his belief that he has come face-to-face with something that cannot be easily explained. Frank first found the courage to come forward and talk about his encounter after seeing a news broadcast that discussed my research into giant flying creatures that have been reported around south Texas. Subsequently, I interviewed him by phone on two separate occasions and then ultimately set up a face-to-face meeting as I was wrapping up work on this very manuscript.

We arranged to commune at a local coffee shop one rainy night in order to compare notes. When we were ordering our lattes, I inadvertently placed my manuscript on the counter, which prompted an inquiry from one of the employees. "What's the deal with Mothman," the young woman inquired. "Is it real?" Without hesitation, Frank looked her in the eye and responded, "I've seen it!"

Frank is a pleasant-looking, soft-spoken person with an air of sophistication about him. Born on Friday the 13th (like myself), he comes across as a very thoughtful and intelligent person who cares deeply about his family. He's worked as a public schoolteacher, wine trader, and is currently pursuing a graduate degree in psychology. Frank admittedly has acquired a taste for the finer things in life despite the fact that he grew up in one of San Antonio's roughest neighborhoods. He confided in me that as a youth, he frequently found himself in situations where he was forced to defend himself, though he somehow managed to avoid the pitfalls of others growing up in his community, instead gravitating towards athletics—boxing and running track. Frank stressed to me that at the time of his encounter he was completely sober and of sound mind.

He remembers the date as being October 18, 1998, three days before a tragic hundred-year flood that resulted in the loss of thirty-two lives in the Alamo City. Frank was in his early twenties at the time, residing with his fiancée at his mother's home on the south side of San Antonio. At around three in the morning, he was saying goodbye to some friends that he had been entertaining that evening. As they drove off, he heard a loud disturbance on his property. Because there had been an attempted burglary at the residence a week prior, Frank crept stealthily into the backyard to investigate, armed with a thick pecan branch he had found on the ground. It was a full, moonlit night, and there seemed to be a deathly calm silence in the air. Even the insects were mute. Frank caught something in his peripheral vision, and when he glanced up, it changed his life forever. As his eyes adjusted to the darkness, he could discern an ominously large black mass that was hovering above him, perched on the roof of the garage.

As Frank describes it, the degree of blackness was staggering, almost as if the object in question was composed of antimatter. He thought at first that the thing might be a gigantic plastic garbage bag, but it seemed to be much larger, at least six feet high. As he tried to make sense of the situation, the mass literally began to come to life and expand, essentially unfurling and growing larger right before his very eyes. What

Frank discerned to be two appendages extended on either side of the thing, and he realized that it was a living entity of some kind. He focused on the area that seemed to comprise its head. From what he could make out, the most unnerving feature was its face, which, although humanlike in nature, was stretched downward so that its elongated, pointy chin resembled the shape of a bird's bill. Its eyes looked dark and sunken.

At that moment, Frank was shaken to the very core of his existence. He immediately turned and ran away as fast as he could, while feeling an ominous sense of complete and utter terror. As he fled down the street, he could hear a sound that he has described as a fluttering, similar to a large sheet flapping in the wind. In his mind the creature seemed to be hovering right above him. As Frank tells it, he ran away so fast that he quickly caught up to his friend's car at the end of the block. They had apparently seen him running toward them in their rearview mirror and, sensing that he was in some type of danger, opened the car door so that he could dive into the backseat. For several minutes, he was unable to express to them exactly what had caused him to flee, as he cried and shook uncontrollably, virtually in a state of total shock.

Eventually, the group mustered up the courage to return to his home and investigate. When Frank noticed a neighbor standing outside in his own yard, he approached the man and asked him if he had seen anything unusual, which the neighbor apparently had not. No sign of the being was any-where to be found, much to their shared relief. For many years, Frank had nightmares about the incident and didn't discuss it much with his family or friends. He only knew that he had experienced something utterly inconceivable and that others who were close to him had a tough time accepting that fact.

He repressed the encounter and kept it all to himself until his mother notified him about a news broadcast that I was appearing on in 2007. Eyewitness Guadalupe Cantu III also appeared on the episode and discussed his own sighing of a man-sized bird in Rangerville, Texas. Sensing that it was time to open up, Frank got in touch with well-known San Antonio reporter Joe Conger, who featured his story on a follow-up broadcast before putting him in touch with me.

As it turns out, Frank is quite a gifted artist and his sketches of the entity he encountered that fateful night are disturbing to say the least. They are literally the kind of im-ages from which nightmares are spawned. He has personally found the exercise to be somewhat therapeutic, as he strug-gles to come to terms with what it was he was confronted by all those years ago. During one interview, he confided in me that his remarkable experience has sent him on a lifelong quest for answers. To his credit, Frank seems to have taken an enlightened approach to the mystery. His curiosity was further peaked by a mysterious e-mail he received following his television interview. An anonymous writer suggested that he read science fiction author Arthur C. Clarke's 1953 book titled *Childhood's End,* which characterizes entities known as Overlords—essentially peaceful aliens who have come to Earth in order to usher in a new age.

This line of thinking led Frank to wonder if the entity was somehow related to the great worldwide mythos of skyborne demigods who go by many names, though they are generally referred to as "watchers." There seems to be a great deal of significance related to the appearance of these legendary beings, though we can only speculate about their true origin and purpose. Frank suggested to me that south Texas possesses some of the most extensive cave systems in the world, a perfect hiding place for a race of rarely seen creatures that only come to the surface on fleeting occasions. But he also made a very poignant statement to me when he pointed out, "There are things going on around us all the time that the human mind is unwilling to accept." Whatever the reason, Frank Ramirez feels that he was chosen.

Flying Humanoid over Long Beach, California

Shortly after my appearance on a television program dealing with the Mexican UFH cases, I was contacted by a writer named Gian Temperelli. At the time, Gian had just finished coauthoring a biography for well-known psychic Peter James and felt the need to share his own personal otherworldly experience with me. "You're never going to believe this," his ardent message began, "yet, I've witnessed a flying human-oid." Temperelli seemed to want to distance himself from the metaphysical nature of James's work, as he further detailed:

> It was about 1990 in Long Beach, California, on the pen-insula where I lived with my parents at the time, just after high school. I rarely take naps. Yet I just awoke from one that I took and looked out my window and saw a man [standing upright] flying fluidly across our alley and over a neighbor's rooftop! IT WAS AS CLEAR AS DAY! It really looked like a superhero; yet I knew it didn't exist. I haven't even thought about it since that first encoun-ter; yet the show [*MonsterQuest*] recalled all that. It was very real. And I even went up to my parent's third-floor deck to see if it was real (or if anyone on the immediate beach saw it) yet discovered nothing, or saw that no one else saw anything. And it was sort of slow moving in a "hovering glider" type apparatus. This was a freestand-ing person [upright] cruising along Ocean Boulevard with no attachments! Haven't seen anything like it since.

It would seem that Temperelli's description matches the figures in the Mexican videos quite well. He later added, "The suit 'skin' color and patina gloss was vibrant and a pol-ished shine."

It is worth noting that I have received recent reports of other unusual flying things within the greater metropoli-tan Los Angeles area, including observations of apparently surviving pterodactyls from prehistoric times, as well as airplane-sized thunderbirds, similar to the great eagles from Native American legends. So unless George Lucas or James Cameron are shooting their latest blockbuster films there, something extraordinary seems to be occurring in the skies over the City of Angels. Considering that Southern California is often perceived as a veritable fantasy world, it all makes sense to me in an amusing sort of way.

Phantom Flyers— Activity in Florida

My friend and colleague, cryptozoologist Scott Marlowe, has investigated several accounts of a winged Floridian specter that has been labeled the Phantom Flyer, although some have also referred to it as the Dixie Demon. While Scott seems to feel that what people are actually seeing is some kind of immense bird, such as an owl (Strigiforme), there is at least one account that has surfaced from the Florida–Georgia border worth addressing here. It all came to light thanks to Mothman researcher Andy Colvin, who met and interviewed a Virginia family that claimed they saw something remarkable while driving north on I-95 in 2001. At the time, eyewitness Ed Oundee was behind the wheel and his mother was riding shotgun while Ed's father slept soundly in the backseat. It was about 2:00 in the morning and the road was noticeably deserted. Ed was running his high beams when simultaneously both he and his mother spotted a large shape floating in the air about a hundred yards ahead of them.

As they approached the object, they observed what appeared to be a large body, similar in shape to a butterfly's but infinitely more massive, weighing at least a couple hundred pounds in their estimation. The thing displayed no extremities or even a discernible head, and its wings were not immediately noticeable to Ed, though his mother saw them right away. They both perceived what appeared to be two distinct red eyes anchored in its physique as they drew closer and passed underneath it. The apparently organic entity seemed much too heavy to be airborne, in their concerted opinion. Ed summed up the unnerving encounter by stating, "It did change my perception of what was out there. I mean I don't believe in monsters. I don't believe in angels or demons. But this thing just blew my mind away. I've told many people and every time I talk about it I get scared. I get chills in my back. And I don't know what to do. I feel like crying."

The incident is corroborated by the fact that I've received word of strange flying noises from the northern Florida city of Jacksonville. Specifically, a man named John Whittet got in touch with me in order to relate how he and his family have heard loud flapping noises just over the roof of their home on multiple occasions. In Whittet's own words, "One night in 2007, my son and I heard something large swoop down and through our trees at approximately 11:30 p.m. And no. I know what you are thinking. It was not a large owl. I have lived here over thirty years, and this had the sound of a large bat flying, but the size of a man. Whatever it was scared

the crap out of my son and me when it landed on the neighbor's roof and let out this blood-curdling scream." According
to Whittet, his son remains fearful to this day.

Even in light of another account from Florida, we cannot
completely rule out Marlowe's mammoth owl theory. Early
in 2004 I received an e-mail from a woman named Linda
Jacobson, who wrote, "I heard this story in my dad's shop
when I was in middle school. I'm forty-three now. A trucker
friend of my dad's had come across Alligator Alley, which
was very different back then from now. He related to my dad
how he had to stop his semi for a big owl that sat in the road.
Back then there were all kinds of stories about big snakes and
big birds, to be followed in latter years by big UFOs over the
glades."

We will explore various theories regarding misidentifications of giant birds, as well as a possible UFO connection in
the concluding chapter.

Maneuvers over
Fort Hood, Texas

In December of 2009, I was contacted by a woman from
Texas named Cherie Ashby. Cherie happens to live on the
Fort Hood Military Base situated less than 150 miles north
of where I currently reside in San Antonio. In a letter to me,
Cherie confessed:

In August of 2007, I saw a flying humanoid. I didn't just see something move fast in the sky. And believe it or not, it was right over Fort Hood. I spent the last few years wondering if it was an army-training thing or something from space. I know I was not the only person who saw what I saw. I was in my car and I pulled over to watch "it." The cars in front of and behind me also stopped and watched.

Here is what I saw. I was driving down a road on Fort Hood, on my way to visit a friend. The car in front of me slowed down and completely stopped in the road. After my brief frustration over their stopping, I saw what had the other driver's attention. I looked up and what I saw was what I thought was a soldier, in BDUs [Battle Dress Uniform] floating about 30 feet over the power lines. It looked as if the "soldier" was wearing a rain poncho. He was low enough to the ground and my car that I was able to see the entire body. I would guess it was 50-60 feet from my car. I rolled down my window expecting to hear some noise coming from the being.

The head was covered with the "hood" of the poncho. What disturbed me so much was that I could see the feet. They looked like they were standing on a flat surface, like an invisible piece of glass. The being floated very slowly. It moved from one side of the road to the other and continued moving/floating slowly across the field that it was now over. It didn't go up or down, just floated from south to north. I tried to describe to people what I saw and most everyone I told laughed at me. I can't say that I blame them. I've asked soldiers about it, thinking there was a new top-secret jet pack or something. Of course I got no answers.

I've held this information for some time and when I saw the
History Channel show, I was excited to know that I was not
the only person to have seen something.

So, an intriguing affirmation that at least a few of these
incidents may in truth be spawned by the military, perhaps
involving some type of experimental flying apparatus that
has been kept top secret. But why then would the device
be tested in plain view of several civilians during the day?
A lengthy phone interview with Cherie seemed to confirm
that she was quite sincere and was more than a little freaked
out by her encounter. In fact, I got the distinct impression
that my extreme interest in her experience served as a form
of validation that provided her with some degree of closure.

Chaparral,
New Mexico's Birdman

Of the handful of flying humanoid narratives that have trick-
led in over the past decade, one of the creepiest has to do
with a winged creature that was seen by a credible eyewitness as recently as 2007, according to an online article that
was posted by researcher Brent Raynes. A native of Tennessee
who has been investigating UFO reports since 1967, Raynes
heads up a magazine and website called *Alternate Perceptions*.
He frequently pens articles having to do with a multitude
of cosmic mysteries ranging from lost civilizations to visitors
from other realms. Raynes also possesses a keen interest in the
Mothman mystery and is an ardent follower of John Keel's

musings. According to Raynes, a gentleman who works for the El Paso, Texas, judicial system related to him how his brother had spotted a humanoid entity as it glided over the desert town of Chaparral, New Mexico. The brother's name is Nicanor Hernandez, and I was able to interview both him and his wife on the phone one evening.

The encounter evidently occurred in the early morning hours of September 14, while Nicanor was lying on the rear trunk of his car, looking up at the stars and chatting with his wife, who was standing nearby. Suddenly he noticed the shadow of an impressive winged beast flying overhead at a height of about forty to fifty feet. The subject was somewhat illuminated by the moon, as well as a nearby streetlight. Because the incident occurred quickly, all Nicanor could make out was that whatever the thing was, it appeared to be completely featherless. Nicanor estimated the creature had a wingspan that rivaled that of a hang glider, about fifteen feet across. He called out to his wife to take a look, but she did not want to have anything to do with the thing and instead rushed into the house. Apparently, in the decades prior, there had been rumblings around Chaparral of a black, manlike entity that had been seen flying over the community on various occasions. In fact, Nicanor confided in me that he and his brother had seen something large shoot over their car some years earlier while driving on a local highway.

Another sighting that was related to me is markedly more dramatic. The incident came to light during a harmless game, whereby neighborhood children attempted to spook each other with scary stories. As a result, Nicanor and his wife learned that his next-door neighbor had also claimed to have seen the Birdman back during the 1980s. The neighbor, who works as a truck driver, had stepped outside for a smoke late one night while battling a bout of insomnia when he noticed an intense disturbance in the adjacent treetops. One tree in particular was swaying back and forth violently as if it were being manipulated by some unseen force. As his dog retreated behind him in fear and began to bark, the neighbor claimed that he observed a man-sized, winged creature standing a mere five to six feet in front of him. He desperately flicked his lighter on in an attempt to get a better look at the thing. This apparently startled the creature, causing it to take off and then land on the roof of Nicanor's garage, leering ominously down at the man and vocalizing for a brief moment before taking off again and flying posthaste into the murk. The aberration continually emitted a bone-chilling shriek that also possessed overtones of a hissing sound, though the entire encounter was over in mere seconds. The witnesses' description of the Birdman was that it was completely featherless and stood at least seven to eight feet tall. It landed like a raptor (feet first) and stood on two legs. It tilted its head like an owl. It possessed wings and also arms with clawed hands. It had a puny head with menacing fangs, but no visible eyes.

My conversation with both Nicanor and his wife confirmed the notion that there had been reports of the Chaparral Birdman dating back decades, including one teenage boy they knew who had observed the being for several minutes. The most recent encounter involved Nicanor's son, who claimed he saw the creature feasting on a road-killed dog carcass while returning from the movies one night.

It is significant that Chaparral is nestled in the part of the United States that is most associated with UFO activity. The site of the famous UFO crash incident near Roswell lies a mere two hundred miles to the northeast (as the man-bird flies), with White Sands Missile Range (sight of the first atomic bomb detonation) nearby. The proximity of the locale to the Mexican border is not surprising in light of what we have learned so far.

In addition, I have collected other reports from the general region, including one from a hiker named David Zander, who told an Albuquerque television station that he spotted two ugly man-sized birds as they perched on a peak in the Dona Ana Mountains. Additionally, a young woman contacted me recently and told me that her family had spotted something that resembled a prehistoric pterosaur gliding near the town of Alto. New Mexico seems to have a proclivity for these types of events, much like its namesake to the south.

On a strictly personal note, my ex-wife and her friend had a disturbing experience not far from Chaparral one summer night in 2004. The three of us were driving from El Paso, Texas, to California at about three in the morning when I was abruptly disturbed from my slumber. Both women seemed visibly hysterical as they explained to me how they had just passed a car-sized object hovering above the road just moments before. Both insisted that the "craft" was completely spherical and smooth in appearance, that it illuminated bright light, and that it seemed to be enveloped in a sort of haze. Despite their apprehension, I attempted to persuade them to turn the car around so I could get a look at the thing myself, which they clearly had no interest in doing. It seems fairly obvious that there is an undeniable link between our flying humanoids and areas of intense UFO activity.

White, Caped Humanoid Seen on Farm in Bucks County, Pennsylvania

Yet another uncanny report I received came from a man named Drew who wrote:

> I am messaging you because I have had a sighting of a humanoid figure in Bucks County, Pennsylvania, near Philadelphia. It was in June 2008 at my local farm. My friend and I were driving at the farm at around 6:30 p.m. We were driving along the cornfields trying to spot deer. As we were passing a clearing between the cornfields we saw the humanoid figure [floating upright] from about 150 yards away. It was all white and appeared to

be in a cape. It was floating about one to two feet off the ground and looked to be four and a half to five feet tall. It was visible for about three seconds, and then it floated into the cornfield. After it disappeared, my friend and I drove to where it passed into the corn and discovered that there was a broken cornstalk. I know for a fact that what I saw is not a known creature or an albino deer.

An eerie encounter indeed! In fact, Drew sums the incident up nicely by pointing out, "I believe that my sighting is unique due to most of the sightings I have heard of have been on the West Coast and in Mexico." Inexplicable events do seem to be afoot in the eastern states as well.

Perhaps not coincidentally, Bucks County was the nexus of intense UFO activity during 2008, yet another strong indicator that there is a connection to some, if not all, of the flying humanoid encounters.

Mothman Encounters in Kentucky

According to cryptozoologist and author Ron Coffey of the Bluegrass State, Pike County in the far eastern part of Kentucky suffered a small outbreak of Mothman-type reports during August of 2008. Ron received his information from an elderly farmer named Israel "Red" Crain, who claimed that he was chased one night by a six-foot-tall, owl-looking creature that shrieked at him while bobbing its head back and forth. Crain told Coffey that the first encounter he had heard about allegedly involved a local woman who was out walking her dog one evening around 10:00. Without warning, the woman's loyal pooch began to act nervou,s and after a moment it became shockingly clear why, as a creature of immense proportions appeared before them in menacing fashion. Coffey's book *Kentucky Cryptids* gives Crain's recollection of the creature: "It stopped and looked straight at me. It had giant, red, glowing eyes, and must have been over seven feet tall. I ran as fast as I could back to the house with the dog howling the whole way."

The monster was supposedly seen later that same evening by a police officer who drove up on the figure as it was standing in the middle of the thoroughfare he was patrolling. When the deputy exited his patrol car to confront what he had assumed to be a man, the entity turned to face him, and the officer realized that it was something freakish in nature. At that point, shots were fired, but they evidently had no effect on the being. Sadly, Coffey tells me that his contact, Mr. Crain, passed away recently.

Despite his reluctance to let his story go public, it is worth retelling here. Still, we must always be cautious with regard to accounts that stem from a single source, and Coffey was unable to track down any of the other witnesses.

Batman Moves
to My Hometown

Throughout the years, I've had the distinct honor of working with the Mutual UFO Network (MUFON). The world's largest and oldest UFO organization, it has investigated reports of unidentified flying objects all over the world for nearly half a century. One of its members is a friend and colleague named Richard West. I owe him a great debt of gratitude for sharing the following case transcript with me. It involves a San Antonio woman with the initials V.R. The incident apparently occurred in April of 2009.

In the witness's own words:

I was talking on my cell at the end of my sidewalk by the street when I turned around facing my house and saw this huge black man-bird thing gliding without a noise coming from the east, maybe the distance would be like three streets over but about maybe five blocks down… When I saw this I was stunned and stared at it trying to figure out what it was, and then I saw it wasn't anything I've ever seen. I ran into the house and yelled at my husband and my grown son to get out here quick. They came but [it] seemed like forever, and they looked and saw it, too. When they saw it, they [sic] thing was like a few streets over and then disappeared behind the big trees.

When we saw it, we all said that no one would believe us; but I have recently been talking about it because it has bothered me so much. I lived in this neighborhood all my life and I can remember three UFO sightings since I was five, and all the sightings were in this neighborhood or around Stinson Field Airport. I never came forward about them because people think ya [sic] lost your ever-loving mind until recently when others I've spoke with shared their experiences. I have other stories, but this one is the most recent, and I was wondering if anyone has ever seen this thing. It is silent like it was a glider, but I could see the body was exactly like a man—a very large man.

The woman's correspondence concludes, "Thank you for listening to me and I hope you don't think we have gone mad, too … I had my darn cell on the whole time and not once thought of taking a picture. It happened so fast and I'm not that savvy on the cell."

Despite the eyewitness's proclivity to avoid both punctuation as well as a follow-up interview by MUFON, we now have ample evidence that accounts like hers are more common than we would like to admit. It makes me wonder how many "experiencers" repress their urge to speak publicly about these events for fear of having a butterfly net cast over their heads. Therefore, the dozens of accounts included in this book may only scratch the surface of this phenomenon.

Sacramento Photographer
Observes a Monster

On an episode of the popular television series *MonsterQuest,*
dealing with the topic of Mothman, the broadcast featured
a testimonial from an eyewitness named Lamont Greer. A
Sacramento, California, native, Greer is evidently a photog-
raphy enthusiast. According to his videotaped interview on
the program, Greer stated that he was out taking pictures of
a suspension bridge late one night in August 2009 and had
just crouched down to put his camera in its case when he
had an eerie feeling. It was then that he glanced up and noticed some kind of object perched high on the bridge. As his
eyes adjusted to the darkness, Greer claimed that he could
make out something animate and weird that appeared to be
alive. Suddenly, whatever the thing was, it spread its wings
and fluttered off into the darkness. Greer explained, "That's
when I could see the extension of the body... It was something that was absolutely strange and something unique."

At the conclusion of the interview, Greer was adamant
that the creature he saw was neither a bird nor a man, but
seemed to be an intermediate between both orders. His
final remarks reinforced his belief that the monster was
large enough to pose a real threat to anyone unfortunate
enough to find themselves in its path: "I mean, if it wanted
to come down and really hurt someone or attack. It absolutely could definitely cause damage."

Why Did the Winged
Humanoid Cross the Road?

One of the most recent reports is also one of the weirdest. It comes courtesy of Stan Gordon of Pennsylvania, a long-time chronicler of UFOs and monsters from the Keystone State. This hair-raising encounter was relayed to Gordon by a traveling businessman who was motoring through Butler County on March 18, 2011. The witness noticed some motion on the right side of the road ahead, and at first he figured that there was a large animal waiting to cross. As he switched on his high beams, the object stood up, and the man realized that the creature was extremely tall, muscular, and manlike in form. While seemingly this may sound like the beginning of a typical Bigfoot encounter, nothing could be further from the truth. I now quote Stan Gordon's summary of the man's description:

> The head appeared to be flat in the front section, and then rounded out. "At the top back of skull, it was like one of those aerodynamic helmets. The top was not quite a point, but looked like a ridge on top of the head." The face was flat, and the eyes were not clearly defined, but the man thought that they might have been pointed in the corner. The ear that was observed on the left side was long and flat, and came up and back and was pointed backwards like a flap. The arms were muscular and a little longer than that of a human. The hands looked more like a claw, but

the number of fingers was unclear. One physical trait that stood out was the extremely muscular legs.

The witness stated that it was hard to explain, but the legs did not move like that of a human and "looked like they bent backwards."

Of course, it is the next detail that truly bears mentioning in this particular work: "The witness also saw what appeared to be wings on its back, which were tucked into its body, with the wing tips extending toward the side of its head." A vivid description to be sure and also thought-provoking as we near the end of our journey. Whatever this eyewitness encountered, it seems to fit nicely into the diverse pantheon of winged weirdos alongside Mothman, Batsquatch, and the rest of John Keel's "trooping faerie menagerie." There is no reasonable conclusion that we can reach when we hear such descriptions. And yet can we simply afford to discard an account based on its singularity, or should we step back and look at the big picture of the flying humanoid enigma, in order to take note of the similarities?

Before we proceed, we should summarize this particular case. The creature in question was in a hunched position when the witness first sighted it, and then it stood up. As he watched it over the course of several seconds, the being crossed the road in three long strides and vanished into the brush on the other side. The man observed that the monster appeared hairless with tan, leathery skin. Based on measurements, the witness took into comparison a road sign that the thing had been standing next to; he determined that the figure stood over eight feet tall.

Kansas City's Winged Demon

A seemingly relevant case that I would like to include is one that arrived on my doorstep via a paranormal investigator from Kansas City, Missouri, who didn't deem herself qualified to draw any conclusions. It involves two sisters who both encountered something that they describe as a kind of demon bird. There are apparently at least four sightings by multiple witnesses and, curiously, the primary contact is a woman named Angel, who confided in me that she happens to be a very devout Christian. I interviewed her and her sister at length over the phone and gleaned the following details.

Their first encounter occurred just two days after the great tragedy of Hurricane Katrina in August of 2005. Angel and her sister live in an area of Kansas City, Missouri, called Swope Park, which lies near the city zoo. As Angel's sister and a male friend were standing out in the yard talking one day, they apparently heard a very loud noise. Looking up, they noticed what they at first took to be a giant bird hopping awkwardly from tree branch to tree branch. As it drew closer, they were able to discern that the "bird" was black in color and truly gigantic in stature, at least the height of a man and displaying a wingspan between twelve and eighteen feet across. The creature possessed batlike wings and leathery skin in addition to a long, curved beak and dark, deep-set eyes. Angel's sister also told me that the apparition possessed a huge head with a face like an "ugly person." Whatever the thing was, it seemed to be attempting to become airborne, though quite unsuccessfully. The observers couldn't help but notice that the entity appeared "wobbly" and unsure in its movements. When the incomprehensible beast eventually landed on their property, the pair frantically scrambled into the house, where Angel's sister collapsed on the floor in a state of shock. The next thing they knew, there was a loud thud on the side of the house, as if the monster had slammed into the side of the wall.

For years, the family tried to forget the terrifying events of that day until April of 2011, when the creature returned. This time it was in the evening, and once again, the monster's appearance was preceded by a strange sound, likened to a dog being choked. The demon bird was then observed cavorting among the streetlights. An inquiry by the family led to word of another incident that involved one of their cousins who claimed that he also saw the thing after leaving their house one night. He had spotted the animal when it hopped behind the taillights of his car, and he observed that it had a fat, round body and a wingspan twenty to twenty-five feet wide. Another neighborhood couple stated they had seen the demon bird on Eastwood Street back in 2000. They swore that it had a humanlike face, but with a beak that had holes (nostrils?) in its side. During my extensive interview, I definitely got the sense that both Angel and her sister were emotionally scarred by their encounters and in dire need of answers. I could provide none.

Return of the
Madisonville Birdman

The final case I will discuss comes hot off the presses and seemingly marks the return of an old, familiar friend. The community of Clinton, Tennessee, lies a mere sixty miles northeast of the city of Madisonville, which we discussed in chapter three with regard to its Birdman stories. A young woman named Lisa Letanosky provided me with the following account, which evidently took place in June 2012. In a heartfelt message to me, Lisa wrote, "I just saw a bird that was the most interesting bird I have ever seen. It was huge. It looked just like a Terradactyl [sic]. It had arms like people arms and there was not fur or feathers on the underside of its belly. There was a huge flap of skin hanging down from under its chin. It left a huge shadow over the house as it flew over. All I could do is say, 'What the [expletive] is that?' The neighbor's kid saw it as well. Very neat."

My follow-up inquiry solicited additional details from Lisa:

I live in a subdivision called Brookestone. It was around maybe 4:00 or 5:00 when he was spotted by me and flew over our home very low, might I add. My brother and neighbor were out here and saw the shadow of it fly over and they were like, "What in the world?" I saw it and the kid across the street saw it as well. It looked like a Terradactyl [sic] from cartoons I used to watch as a child. It was large but looked to be a baby . . . small head, long flap of skin under its neck. Belly looked to be the skin of a dragon like you see in the science fiction movies. Its arms were spread out, but it brought them in once, and you could see the skeleton of its arms. They looked like people arms, kinda. This all happened so fast. I ran to the backyard to see it again, but we have a lot of trees back there, and it was already gone. I'm not one to say I saw something if I didn't. I'm as shocked as anyone to know this kind of bird actually exists.

Despite Lisa's characterization of the creature as a bird or something akin to a prehistoric winged reptile, it is her description of its humanlike arms that seems to indicate she may have seen something else entirely.

Prehistoric devil birds, leather-skinned batmen and caped humanoids floating freely through the air; it would be easy for a skeptical intellect to ask how these varied descriptions could possibly bear any relevance when grouped together in a collection such as this book. But upon closer examination, there do appear to be some commonalities that are worth discussing in depth. For example, there has been some corroboration in terms of physical characteristics that seem to be recurring within our general groupings. The same could be said for some of the behavior patterns observed. More notably, the locations where flying anomalies have been encountered are fairly consistent—UFO hotspots, military installations, etc. But the most significant aspect is the fear and lifelong emotional trauma that has been experienced by those who have had sightings.

Now that we have had an opportunity to review a diverse anthology of reports that spans almost two centuries, it is time to compile our data and attempt to make sense of it all.

CONCLUSIONS

Cryptozoologists, much like conventional scientists, aim to place their subjects into neat and tidy categories by classifying them within the accepted taxonomic system. In this manner, we can form conclusions about a creature's true origin and nature and determine its potential relationships to known species. In the case of something like Bigfoot/Sasquatch or the Yeti (though admittedly a remarkable proposition), we can examine fossils of different archaic hominoids and speculate that such beings could have potentially avoided total extinction, roaming the remote and unexplored corners of our planet in small but viable numbers. Similarly, the Loch Ness Monster, Great Sea Serpent, and other denizens of the deep bear similarities to marine animals that lived millions of years ago. Yet with regard to something like flying humanoids, we are treading dangerously far beyond the accepted laws of evolution and the natural world. The point being that, in my business, we deal primarily in flesh, blood, and bones ... and it should be blatantly obvious by now that it does not appear that we are dealing with physical specimens in this particular instance, despite the bestial characteristics of some entities contained within this compendium.

From a purely skeptical point of view, the most pragmatic conclusion would be that all of the accounts in this book are fictional—tall tales, intentional fabrications, or hoaxes that were concocted for an assortment of reasons. It is certainly a characteristic of humans to embellish and bedazzle in order to get attention or merely to make life more interesting. The motives are often hard to understand, but they typically revolve around an individual's desire to achieve a certain feeling of self-satisfaction by appearing to be unique or more enlightened than peers.

I will concede that some of the reports listed in these pages are undoubtedly fabricated, primarily those that were put into print with the express purpose of generating a profit. But how do we account for the intense anxiety displayed by many of the modern eyewitnesses, several of whom were said to be hospitalized for post-traumatic stress disorder following their encounters? Remember, too, that many of these individuals were so shaken by their experiences that they promptly reported the encounters to the police. Surely no one of sound mind would risk legal consequences that might stem from such an extreme action. Nor should we forget the severe stigma attached to these types of stories. Why would individuals knowingly subject themselves to the kind of ridicule that is typically endured for making patently improbable or even unimaginable claims?

We might then consider the possibility that some eyewitnesses were merely suffering from a form of acute dementia or perhaps hallucinating these occurrences due to some type of psychological condition. I can tell you that I have had much personal experience with people who appear to be demented, to the extent that some have concocted elaborate fantasy worlds where scores of improbable entities traipse about their property, traveling through inter-dimensional doorways. These individuals are relatively easy to diagnose, since the events seem to center around them alone, with no corroborating evidence. In addition, these fantasy-prone personalities frequently display signs of acute paranoia, and they often ramble on about topics that bear no relevance to anyone but them. I've found that these types have a powerful need to be the center of attention and often live very mundane and lonely lives. Few if any of our eyewitnesses would conceivably fit this profile. By and large, they have been ordinary, upstanding people, living productive and social lives, though frequently having some interest in the unexplained. On this point, it could be argued that some of us are indeed more intuitive, perceptive, or in tune with ambiguous vibrations or levels of activity in our universe, more likely to let inexplicable things pass through our perception filters.

The hallucination theory possesses merit on a couple of levels. For conspiracy theorists, a palpable explanation is that eyewitnesses were the unwilling victims of some sort of covert mind-control experiments, most likely undertaken by the C.I.A., military, or other secretive government organization. It's been documented that the U.S. Army has performed such experiments on its own soldiers by administering hallucinogenic drugs like LSD in order to see how it could potentially disrupt the effectiveness of enemy forces. In addition, author Nick Redfern has uncovered classified documents that outlined a plan by British military intelligence to test a twelve-foot-tall robotic monster (essentially an animatronic scarecrow) by letting it run amok in an isolated village, thereby inducing mass hysteria and chaos. It's not difficult to perceive how an episode like the one that transpired in Point Pleasant would have unfolded at the height of the Cold War, as the result of diabolical experimentation by shadowy Svengalis intent on carrying out some inconceivable agenda.

Yet another possibility worth considering is that there is a valid psychological condition whereby otherwise ordinary, perfectly sane people can experience vivid hallucinations under the right conditions. We must not forget that the human mind is a vastly complex organ that operates on levels we do not always understand. We are particularly prone to hallucinate when our minds are in the twilight phase following sleep. In this state, our logical minds are not always able to differentiate between what is real and imagined. This suggestion seems to falter when we consider mass-witness sightings. However, some psychiatrists, including the great Carl Jung, have speculated that we are all part of a collective human consciousness with shared ingrained memories and belief systems.

We have shown that the premise of flying humanoids is one that dates back thousands of years in the human psyche. Moreover, it has been proven that the power of suggestion in social groups can be quite contagious. Therefore, a mass hallucination shared by several individuals is not totally out of the question. Furthermore, some researchers have hypothesized that images born from deep in our unconscious minds can even manifest and take on physical attributes, essentially thought-projection holograms. The pertinent question is whether or not these things stem from us, or whether there is some external intelligence involved.

We should not discount the possibility that at least some of the encounters are merely cases of mistaken identity. Misinterpretation is an unfortunate result of our human fallibility when it comes to our perception of certain types of events. Heisenberg's Uncertainty Principle effectively illustrates that we have severe shortcomings when it comes to relying solely on our senses, in addition to processing information with accuracy in real time. I imagine this is especially true when our adrenaline is pumping and our imagination is running wild.

Some obvious examples of mistaken identity might include the hovering men that have been sighted over Mexico and elsewhere. For decades, governments and inventors around the globe have experimented with top-secret flying platforms and jet packs. It's not hard to conceive of a scenario where unknowing civilians might have jumped to remarkable conclusions about what they were observing. However, I don't give much credibility to theories that suggest misidentifications of common birds like owls being possible explanations. While this could conceivably occur on very rare occasions, owls and other large birds do not display even the slightest humanoid characteristics, nor do they come anywhere close to being manlike in size.

So, assuming that there is validity to some of the accounts and that these airborne entities actually do exist, let's take a look at patterns, something I'm always eager to do.

One of the more obvious aspects of the mystery is the wide variation of flying humanoids that have been described within these pages. The major types include anthropomorphic hybrids between humans and birds, such as Mothman and Owlman. These seem to display a generally human-shaped form but also possess wings and sometimes feathers, talons, or other avian characteristics. As I've inferred throughout the course of this book, this is quite impossible, anatomically speaking. One needs only to revisit Da Vinci's ornithopter experiments or consider the parable of Icarus to discount this notion. Men and wings simply don't mix.

In a similar vein, the second category of man-bat hybrids, despite mammalian characteristics, are problematic for the same reasons, unless we are willing to entertain the possibility of a heretofore unrecognized gargantuan species of bat. The third major category includes our wingless aeronauts, a relatively late arrival on the scene and presumably reliant on artificial means in order to remain airborne.

Of course, not all of the creatures contained within these pages fit into any of these three groups, which is problematic to say the least. I would suggest that the gargoyle and chimera types generally belong in either of our first two classes, depending on whether their wings are visibly feathered or membranous. As we can see, there are just far too many variations to make sense of it in scientific terms.

Perhaps, therefore, more clarity can be achieved by considering the similarities instead of the differences. This is best done from an anthropological perspective. The one clear denominator in all of the cases is the human element. After all, without a person or persons to experience and react to this phenomenon, its significance would be hard to measure. I can think of no better use of the solitary tree falling in the forest metaphor. Consider again the profound emotional impact that these experiences have on the observer and the symbolism of what they represent to us in the big picture.

Next, let's take a look at the demographics of the individuals involved. It's worth noting that the majority of flying humanoid eyewitnesses seems to be younger people, particularly females. An obvious example is Cornwall's Owlman, where virtually every sighting was logged by a teenage girl, except one where a young Gavin was present. Most of Mothman's pivotal witnesses were younger women, including Linda Scarberry, Marcella Bennett, and Connie Carpenter. There are possible reasons for this. It has been suggested that young people are more perceptive or open-minded to things that do not fit neatly into our frame of reference. It is true that as we get older we tend to develop filters based on our view of the world around us. These blinders often color our perception as we become set in our ways. When something inexplicable occurs that makes us uncomfortable, we draw upon our experience in order to develop a rational explanation that we can live with, or else live in denial for fear that something can damage the foundation that we have built our lives upon.

Taking this to another level, females may be more intuitive than males, the result of their nurturing and protective instincts. They don't have as many filters to sift through as males and are generally more in touch with their emotions.

Another key component worth considering is location. It seems that these apparitions frequently have a specific haunt if they are seen more than once. For Mothman, it was the TNT Area; for Owlman, the grounds surrounding Mawnan

Church. The Jersey Devil roams the entirety of New Jersey's Pine Barrens, and the Brentford Griffin was spotted by witness Kevin Chippendale from approximately the same exact spot, albeit months apart. Mexico, California, Texas, England, and Russia are a few of the sovereign regions that these beings call home on a regular basis. To me, this implies a supernatural component, since certain places seem to generate weird energies and ghostly activity. Some researchers have suggested that there are specific "gateways" or "window" areas, that open or connect to other dimensions of reality...pretty heavy stuff!

Ultimately, I've been investigating the flying humanoid phenomenon for a number of years now, and the only solid conclusion I have come to is that these beings, whatever they are, wherever they are from, are not flesh and blood—at least not in a way that we understand it. Furthermore, they seem to have an intense need to interact with humans by utterly terrifying us, feeding off of our fear like psychic vampires. Young people, particularly females, would make superior targets, since surging hormones and their resulting emotions are plentiful. Consider all of the accounts of these beings chasing people at impossible speeds and moving in impossible ways, the fact that they vocalize in an aggressive and disturbing way, and their hypnotic, glowing eyes as well as alleged physical attacks. Consider the rancid smells associated with their presence and the fact that to have an encounter with one can cause an individual to feel violently ill or to have residual psychological trauma and nightmares that can last for years. They are the manifestation of evil incarnate, and they are drawn to us.

It is easy to relate this model to the cross-cultural myths that portray these entities as very bad omens, harbingers of disaster, and bringers of death. Perhaps owls and bats were merely the victims of a blame game. For whenever the winged, humanoid phantoms disappeared back into the void from whence they came, humans had to make sense of the legends, and these nocturnal animals seemed to best represent our fear of the darkness... of the unknown. Owls are, after all, imposing, predatory birds that reign supreme during the darkness of night, emitting eerie, piercing shrieks.

In a similar vein, bats have been made into monsters in the minds of many. While they are admittedly hideous-looking, they are generally harmless to humans, except, of course, for the vampire variety. Both types of animals are merely scapegoats, misunderstood minions of the night, and they most assuredly do not explain the widespread mythology of winged humanoids.

I find the link to UFOs most compelling. Particularly when we contemplate the ancient accounts of airborne gods from the heavens that are prevalent in so many cultures. A multitude of flying humanoid episodes seem to be accompanied by UFO activity. Point Pleasant was inundated with lights in the sky during Mothman's primary reign, Houston's Batman was seemingly spirited away by a torpedo-shaped object, and aeronauts were hovering around the skies of Washington State and Mexico following major UFO flaps.

For prognosticators of extraterrestrial conspiracies, this seems like a slam dunk. Our flying humanoids are merely visitors from another world, and their historical presence here is far beyond the realm of human comprehension. Let's expand on this line of thinking and attempt to connect the dots.

It's easy to understand why Mothman investigator and author John Keel came to the conclusion that there is a connection between flying humanoids and other inexplicable phenomena. Based on his own personal experiences, in addition to those of many Point Pleasant residents that he grew to know well, Mothman, UFOs, Men in Black, disembodied voices, and the bridge tragedy were all part of a much grander synopsis with global implications. Keel envisioned a mechanism that he referred to as the "cosmic joker," in essence an ultra-terrestrial intelligence that has been with us since time began—a complex, multi-faceted enigma that chooses to interact with humanity by toying with us in a series of incomprehensible scenarios. This construct seems to be capable of manifesting in a variety of forms and is the root cause of all our enduring mysteries, from ghost and spirit activity to UFOs and the army of nonsensical creatures that have paraded through our world for millennia. Keel referred to this army as the trooping faerie menagerie, and it included all of our impossible and mythological creatures, man-beasts, and the rest. This order would of course also include the flying humanoids.

I will attempt to expound upon this line of thinking while putting it into more scientific terms. Keel was, after all, a self-professed demonologist and felt compelled to view the world with a spiritualist microscope. I, on the other hand, do not at all profess to be a quantum physicist, though I grasp the most basic concepts.

We know that there is energy coursing throughout the universe in a variety of forms and at a molecular level. We also know that there exists a delicate balance to all tangible things as opposing forces offset each other by creating resistance, positive against negative. So, too, are all life forms (including humans) composed of energy, seemingly powered by a series of minute chemical reactions. In a sense, we may also be transistors or conduits, if you will, streaming the energy of the universe through our very beings. There is positive and negative energy within us, as with most matter. I choose to view the flying humanoids as a manifestation of the negative energy that courses through everything, somehow channeled by us and then projected onto a screen that comprises the fabric of our reality.

One needs only to contemplate the outcome of this process. These beings shake us to the very core of our existence. They seem to appear and resonate in places fraught with repugnant undertones. The TNT Area, Mothman's favorite haunt, was at one time a place where ammunitions and explosives—devices intended to kill, maim, and wreak havoc—were manufactured in massive quantities. Centuries earlier, the native peoples viewed the region as a cursed place, perhaps sensing that it was destined for ill-advised purposes. Cornwall's Owlman has always been observed in the woods around Mawnan Church, which apparently rests in an area of intense paranormal activity, built upon an ancient earthwork. Who knows what diabolical energy lies beneath it? Perhaps someday we will have definitive answers. But for now we must continue to look and wonder.

As we reach the end of our extraordinary journey, I must confess that upon reflection, I feel extremely fortunate to have lived such an adventurous and interesting life so far. I've climbed the lofty and mystical peaks surrounding the Inca ruins of Machu Picchu, communed with primitive tribes in the Amazon Basin's emerald jungles, scaled Australia's monolithic Ayers Rock amidst a vast and barren desert, knelt before Thailand's Golden Buddha, and wandered the mist-shrouded shores of Loch Ness, Scotland, in search of a monster. I've taken it all in—all the while maintaining a childlike wonderment about the world around me.

When I was a young lad, my courageous and creative mother used to place me firmly on her lap and captivate me with strange tales of West Virginia's Mothman. My young imagination would race as I contemplated this remarkable notion. Could such a fabulous and terrifying creature actually exist? Surely the planet Earth in all of its expansive splendor could shroud any number of unimaginable beasts, I concluded. If this book has served to open up just one reader's mind to the possibilities, has encouraged just one person to maintain a childlike sense of wonderment like mine, then this exceptionally weird excursion has been well worth it.

APPENDIX

Winged Beings in Mythology and Folklore

The Birdman of Lascaux

The conceptual synthesis of human and avian characteristics can be traced back at least 17,300 years. According to carbon dating, that's the age of the cave paintings at Lascaux, France. Discovered in 1940, an intricate web of caverns there contain illustrations that can be attributed to stone-age Paleolithic humans who immortalized their Ice Age lifestyle with vivid accuracy. Of the some two thousand images, many of the drawings depict animals that the artists were familiar with, such as wild horses and bison. But perhaps the most famous and controversial image is one that portrays a humanlike figure with the head of a bird. The subject seems to have fallen in front of a charging buffalo with a marauding woolly rhinoceros nearby. The Birdman also displays what appears to be an erect phallus, and he has only four fingers on his hands.

The illustration, which lies in a hidden chamber known as The Well, has long been the subject of much conjecture with regard to its true meaning. Some have theorized that the Birdman represents a spirit guide or perhaps a shaman dressed in ceremonial garb and in an "ecstatic trance." But shamanistic practices are believed to have evolved much later in human culture. The spirit-bird symbolism does make sense, since flight often represents a journey up to the heavens, particularly after death. A recent study has proposed a more pragmatic theory. Evidently, the primary outline of the Birdman and buffalo correspond with the constellations of Gemini and Orion, indicating that early men may have engaged in a form of star mapping and astrology. Regardless of its purpose, we must concede that the image stands as a testament to man's fixation with man-bird hybrids, dating back at least seventeen millennia.

Apkallu

In ancient bas-reliefs from the ninth century BC, we can observe Sumerian representations of beings known as the Apkallu or Abgal. While they are frequently characterized as humanlike, they usually display striking, animal-like features, too. In some engravings, the Apkallu are portrayed as winged men with long beards while in others they possess the heads of birds resting atop humanoid bodies. The Apkallu were generally regarded as demigods, sages, priests, and protectors. Their images adorned royal palaces and were strategically placed in corners where evil spirits were said to dwell. It was believed that their origin dated back to the beginning of time, when they were conceived by the great god Enki.

It is also worth mentioning the Annunaki, which are associated with the Babylonian myth of creation. The Annunaki (which included Enki) were tall, humanlike deities who were said to come from the sky, planting the seeds of humanity on our planet and overseeing our development. Some modern theorists have attempted to explain the Annunaki as extraterrestrials that visited Earth thousands of years ago, perhaps aiding in the rapid development of human civilization around that time by altering the genes of primitive hominids like Neanderthals. One diabolical postulation suggests that the Annunaki came from an unknown tenth planet in our solar system and that they created Homo sapiens merely as a form of slave labor. In this disturbing scenario, we humans are essentially an experiment gone awry.

"Pazuzu Rendering" © Ginger Bertline

Pazuzu

Possibly the most odious winged entity is the Assyrian king of wind demons known as Pazuzu or Zu, the bringer of disaster and inclement weather. Strangely ambiguous, Pazuzu is characterized in fetishes as a sort of chimera that blends a human form with a dog's head, two sets of attached wings, talons, and a scorpion's tail. He is typically displayed with his right hand held upright. Spawned by Hanbi, the sun god, some have interpreted Pazuzu as being a protector and punisher of evil. In fact, it is said that in one epic battle, he drove the female demon Lamashtu back to the underworld from whence she came. It seems that the Assyrians didn't always draw a clear line between good and evil. Pazuzu was immortalized as the ultimate antagonist in the fictional horror anthology *The Exorcist*.

Angels

Everyone knows that angels are universally regarded as higher spiritual beings, God's ambassadors that have been sent down to Earth in order to enlighten and protect humankind. But it would appear that the whole notion of angels as winged beings stems largely from medieval artistic interpretation, as opposed to Biblical descriptions. As it is not my objective to dissect the rather complex subject of angels and their true origin and meaning, I will defer to the countless other researchers and theologists who have dedicated entire volumes to their true nature. Though, I do feel that it is quite necessary to mention the Chayyot.

In the Old Testament of the Bible, there is an account of a divine vision that involved the great Hebrew prophet Ezekiel. He described in great detail how a golden chariot called the Merkabah had appeared in the sky before him. One translation states:

> And from the midst was the form of four Chayyot (Living
> Creatures). This was their form—They had a human form.
> Each one had four faces and every one had four wings.
>
> Their feet were straight, and the soles of their feet were
> like those of a calf's foot, and they shined like a vision of
> polished copper. Human hands were under their wings on
> all four sides, and all four had faces and wings. Their wings
> were joined to each other, and they did not turn when they
> went. Each one moved in the direction of their faces when
> they went. The form of their faces were the face of a man,
> with the face of a lion to the right of the four, the face of an
> ox to the left of the four, and also the face of an eagle.
>
> Their faces and wings were separated on top.

An interesting description to be sure! Ezekiel believed these creatures to be angels that had been dispatched by God as a revelation and testament to his almighty power.

Harpies

The most recognizable winged humanoids are undoubtedly the Harpies of Greek Mythology. This can easily be ascribed to the fact that Harpies are featured villains in some of the world's great classic works of literature, including *The Odyssey*, *The Aeneid, Jason and the Argonauts*, and even Dante's *Inferno* from the *Divine Comedy*. In addition, they have been portrayed prominently in cinema, television programs, books, and other realms of popular culture. Harpies are typically regarded as filthy, foul-smelling, winged female monsters with razor-sharp talons. Their anatomy combines the head, flowing locks, and breasts of a hideous, pale-faced hag attached to the feathered body of a vulture or eagle. They may or may not be shown to have arms in addition to wings.

In Greek, the word *Harpy* or *harpyiai* means "snatcher," and according to legend, the modus operandi of these ravenous creatures involves stealing food from the banquet tables of nobility, including Phineus, King of Thrace, as well as the Trojan hero Aeneas. Whatever scraps they leave behind are said to be rendered inedible due to a rancid stench. Harpies are often confused with Sirens, which were also portrayed as woman-bird hybrids in later works of art and fiction. But the traditional view of Sirens was that they were seafaring beings akin to mermaids. Comparable entities include the Greek Erinyes or Furies, as they are referred to in Roman mythology. These vengeful beings are typically summoned to punish those who have committed a great injustice.

Icarus

Another myth from Ancient Greece tells the tragic story of man's first attempt to become birdlike by artificial means. Icarus was the son of Daedalus, an Athenian inventor who had been imprisoned on the island of Crete for aiding the hero Theseus in his quest to slay the monstrous man-bull known as the Minotaur. Daedalus subsequently hatched an escape plan. He fashioned wings for both him and his son using feathers and wax so that they could both take to the air. But on their journey to freedom, the brazen Icarus was so enthralled by his newfound ability to fly that he strayed off course and shot up into the sky. It was there that he got too close to the sun, causing the wax to melt away and the feathers to fall from his wings. Ultimately, Icarus fell from the sky into the sea and drowned. While the parable says a lot about the dangers of blind ambition, it may have also served another purpose. Perhaps it was an attempt to explain the belief in winged men, an ideal that had sprung up in many civilizations up to that point.

"Sphinx Rendering" © Ginger Bertline

Sphinx

Though not necessarily a flying humanoid in the traditional sense, Egypt's Sphinx certainly bears mentioning as well. It stands to reason that if ancient Middle Eastern and Mediterranean cultures worshipped airborne spirits and demigods, this relatively neighboring African empire would mirror that motif to some extent. The Sphinx was considered to be a guardian of sorts, and like the Apkallu, its image was typically found sitting sentry over important places. The Sphinx's appearance seems to have evolved over the centuries, but the traditional interpretation consisted of a human head resting atop the body of a lion, though in many renditions it also possessed the wings of a great bird. Additionally, the prominent Egyptian deity Horus was frequently presented as a humanlike form with the attached head of a falcon, and the comparable god Thoth combined a human form with the head of an ibis bird. The ancient Egyptians were prone to combining both human and all manner of animal features with regard to their idols.

Garuda

In Hindu and Buddhist culture, Garuda is an exceptionally important figure. Often presented as a gargantuan bird with mile-long wings, Garuda is usually adorned with humanlike features as well. For example, his body is frequently characterized as essentially manlike, despite the fact that he is covered with golden feathers and occasionally a bird's head or beak. He plays differing roles, as both a protector and a destroyer.

The first mention of Gardua occurs in the narrative *Mahabharata,* where the creature is hatched from a fiery egg following a gestation period of 150 years. According to common belief, Garuda's mother is enslaved by her sister, the queen of serpents, or *nāgas*. The *nāgas* are Garuda's sworn enemies, as well as his primary source of sustenance. In order to obtain his mother's freedom, Garuda embarks on a quest to obtain an elixir for everlasting life, known as the Amrita. Following a confrontation with the hero Vishnu, the two strike a bargain whereby Garuda becomes Vishnu's mount as the warrior rides into battle. In exchange, Garuda receives the gift of immortality. While the interpretations vary from India to Malaysia, the prevalent theme of a great man-bird remains consistent.

Tengu

In Japanese folklore, the Tengu are mischievous and sometimes dangerous forest spirits that combine a mixture of human and birdlike characteristics. The earliest references to the Tengu can be traced back to stories from the ninth century AD. In his compendium *The Great Yokai Encyclopedia: The A–Z of Japanese Monsters*, my colleague Richard Freeman summarizes:

> One of the best known of all Yokai, the Tengu is a man/bird hybrid. It has two basic forms, the first being a creature with the head of a bird (usually a raven or a bird of prey), a humanoid body, bird's talons and bird's wings. It is known as the Karasu Tengu.

Freeman points out that "Tengu seem invariably male." He goes on to explain that the Yamabushi type are noticeably more humanlike and display a long nose shaped like a beak.

There are many tales of these tricksters interacting with humans and sometimes even causing their deaths. The Tengu are frequently said to be Buddhist monks that have fallen from grace, or noble men and aristocrats whose vanity got the best of them. Ultimately, a curse transforms certain types of men into these beings as a sort of penance. There are also accounts of Tengu aiding humans in distress or joining them in various forms of merriment, such as dancing. As to their true origin, Freeman writes:

> Tengu may have grown out of early bird deities venerated by the Japanese aboriginals...These bird men are found in the legends of many Asian countries.

Indeed, there may be a connection between the legends of both Tengu and Garuda. It seems reasonable to assume that the belief in anthropomorphic avians migrated across the Old World over the course of centuries.

Camazotz

While accounts of winged humanoid entities abounded in various ancient Eastern civilizations, there were parallel notions developing half a world away in the Americas. The Zapotec and Maya people of Mexico and Central America worshipped a much-feared deity known as Camazotz, or Zotz, the "Death Bat." Credited with beheading the folk hero Hunahpu after a great conflict, Camazotz combined the features of bat and man equally and was typically associated with bloodshed and sacrifice. It is curious that engravings of what appear to be man bats can be found at the ruins of Copán in western Honduras.

Farther to the north, in the arid deserts of New Mexico, archaeologists have discovered a Hopi adobe pueblo village dated to the fourteenth century known as Pottery Mound. Within some of the habitations there, one can observe colorful paintings on the walls, some of which seem to represent manlike figures with wings attached to their backs.

Ikals

Deep amidst the emerald jungles of Mexico's Chiapas lies a genuine lost world. In fact, an elderly woman who lived in the area once told me that there are sizeable prehistoric beasts there that still remain hidden from modern science. This remote and mysterious region has long been the domain of the Tzeltal people, indigenous Mayan descendants who still inhabit the Chiapas to this day.

The Tzeltals have many colorful myths, one of which tells of the cave-dwelling Ikals. Likened to tiny, hairy, black men. It is said that Ikals also display batlike features, specifically leathery wings. These creatures are much feared by the Tzeltal tribe because it is believed that if given the opportunity, they will abduct and impregnate human women. In

fact, there is even one story about an especially antagonis-
tic Ikal that was confronted and killed by several Tzeltal
warriors bearing machetes.

"Orang-bati Rendering" © Jon Huston

Orang—bati

Cryptozoologist and author Karl Shuker has written about creatures similar to the Ikals that stem from the Indonesian jungle-island of Seram. Known as the Orang-bati, which translates to "Man Bat," these monstrosities have occasionally been described as resembling orangutans with leathery wings or even as red, furry, flying monkeys. According to Shuker, the local Moluccans have tales about women and children who have been abducted by these manlike monsters that make their home in a dormant volcano named Mount Kairatu. Some skeptics have made a case that the Orang-bati legend can be traced to a tribe of the same name that perpetuated the myth of flight in order to frighten their enemies. In either case, it would seem that remote Seram would be the ideal haunt for an undiscovered beast. The neighboring island nation of Java plays host to a similar flying monster known as the Ahool, which has been likened to a giant bat or perhaps a winged primate.

Popobawa

Across the Indian Ocean from Seram lies the African island of Pemba. Here we find stories of an evil spirit or shapeshifter known as the Popobawa. The meaning of the word is "bat-wing," and similar to its counterparts, the Popobawa is blamed for nocturnal attacks on villagers. In fact, the gruesome nature of this apparition is truly revealed when we learn that the Popbawa is particularly fond of sexual assaults on humans and that it emits a horrific odor that turns the stomach.

What is truly chilling is the fact that a number of alleged Popobawa encounters occurred as recently as 1995, resulting in a mass panic that spread to mainland Africa, including the nearby nation of Tanzania.

Kikiyaon

In African folklore, this heinous and fanciful demon is characterized as resembling a great owl, combined with some humanlike traits. The name literally translated means "soul cannibal," and its descriptions are as foreboding as the Dark Continent itself. Said to possess the head of a Strigiforme with a very large beak, its talons are razor sharp and it possesses deadly spurs on the joints of its wings. Covered in greenish-gray feathers or fur, the Kikiyaon's legs are said to be sturdy and it sports human arms in addition to wings. Other distinct traits include its smell, said to resemble a dead serpent that has been lying in the sun, and its mournful cry, which has been likened to the sound of a person being strangled to death!

Faeries

The mention of faeries conjures up whimsical visions of wispy, butterfly-winged spirits flitting about an enchanted forest. Like angels, there is a vast culture dedicated to the interpretation and glorification of these magical beings, and, like angels, their wings seem to have evolved through artistic imagination rather than spoken or written descriptions.

Though, in many fables, faeries are endowed with magical powers, including the ability to fly. The best way to disentangle the state of affairs would be to pronounce that there seems to be a complex taxonomic system involved, and the designation Faerie represents the largest classification or phylum. Distinct sub-orders that include elves, pixies, goblins, gnomes, trolls, and many others certainly make for a fanciful discussion but do not specifically suit our purpose here. Still, we may be able to uncover some clues if we examine the faerie folklore of various European cultures.

Swan Maidens

In a handful of European countries, there are colorful myths about shapeshifting apparitions known as the Swan Maidens. From Germany to Sweden and Romania there exist disparate fairy tales about these beings, though there are some recurring themes. The basic idea is that they are beautiful women who are able to transform into swans with the aid of an enchanted gown made of feathers. It is said that if a man is looking for a wife, he can stealthily snatch the gown while a Swan Maiden is bathing in the nude and thus persuade her to remain with him while transfixed in her human state.

Skovman

Scandinavian folklore features a creature known as the Skovman, reputed to be an elf that is capable of transforming into a colossal owl.

"*Alkonost Rendering*" © *Ginger Bertline*

Alkonost

In Russian and Slavic legends, there is a Sirenlike entity known as the Alkonost.

Similar in appearance to a Harpy but possessing instead the face of a gorgeous woman attached to a large bird, this creature is said to sing so beautifully that those who hear her "forget all that they know." Another intriguing fact regarding the Alkonost's reproductive cycle is that it is said she lays her eggs on a beach before rolling them into the sea. Supposedly, when the eggs hatch, it creates impassible storms that sailors must weather. Other names for this creature include Gamayun and Sirin. These are undoubtedly adaptations of the Greek Siren myth.

Skree

During Scotland's infamous Battle of Culloden Moor, there was apparently a remarkable incident that took place. The date was April 15, 1746, and a regiment of British soldiers under the command of the Duke of Cumberland were looking to suppress an uprising of Jacobite rebels attempting to overthrow the House of Hanover. The Scots were championing their challenger, Bonnie Prince Charlie. On the eve before the battle, it is said that a gigantic, black, birdlike creature appeared and flew over the disbelieving Jacobite troops led by Lord George Murray. The creature, known as the Skree, let out a horrific cry as it soared overhead. The apparition was subsequently described as resembling a Harpy, with glowing red eyes and leathery wings. The Skree's arrival no doubt was intended to be a warning, since the Jacobites were slaughtered in a bloody battle the next day, losing some 1,500 men. This particular incident (if more than a tall tale) is perhaps our first indicator that there is a link between accounts of flying humanoids and calamities.

Furthering this notion is the next Skree appearance, which may have taken place during World War I, according to Karl Shuker in his book *From Flying Toads to Snakes With Wings.* Shuker explains:

> It reputedly appeared in the sky above a 500-strong group of Royal Scots men and officers about to catch a train at Larbert Railway Station that would begin their journey to the Flanders fields. Alarmed by such an ill omen, the men had to be forced at gunpoint by their officers to mount the train. The train crashed later that same day and caught fire, killing 227 passengers and injuring 246 more.

Gwrach−y−rhibyn

In Welsh folklore we find tales of the Gwrach-y-rhibyn, also known as the "Night Hag" or "Slobber Witch." She is said to be a vile, swarthy, corpselike witch who flies low over the water. Gwrach-y-rhibyn is often adorned in black flowing robes. In some stories, she has grown batlike wings and has withered arms as well as long black fangs. To encounter her is considered exceptionally poor luck, since her appearance is thought to be a portent of death. In fact, Gwrach-y-rhibyn will sneak up on poor, unsuspecting peasants and shriek in their ears, or sometimes call out their name, spelling out their doom. Similarities to the Skree in terms of both physical description and geographic proximity certainly bear mentioning.

Bird Woman of Minehead

In Peter Marshall's book *Mother Leakey and the Bishop: A Ghost Story*, Marshall writes of—

> An eye-opening report in the 2004 edition of the New Zealand Cornish Association Newsletter about "the Bird-Woman of Minehead"—an old witch supposed to have the power to transform herself into a strange cormorant-like bird, which would fly to the top of the ship's masts and screech abuse at sailors.

Marshall summarizes by stating, "This creature, we are told, was still being seen well into the twentieth century."

As far as I am aware, this is the only flying humanoid reference from either the island of New Zealand or the neighboring continent of Australia.

Lechuza

Another similar being in Mexican culture is Lechuza, a *bruja*, or witch, that uses dark magic in order to transform into the form of a great bird or birdlike monster. There seem to be varied interpretations of this legend, particularly since the word "lechuza" is synonymous with the name for owl. A young Texan once told me that Lechuza perches in a tree and whistles at passersby. Though, it is common knowledge that to answer her back can be quite treacherous. Since the story is so prevalent in my home of south Texas, I decided to ask several friends to relate their own versions to me, as told to them by their parents.

One San Antonio resident related to me that his parents had told him Lechuza was a bird with an ugly woman's head and that if you hear her scream, you will die within the year. An older Mexican gentleman explained to me that a scary black bird, like an eagle, had been shot near the village where he grew up, and it was said that when the body was recovered, it had transformed into a woman who was widely known to be a witch by the locals.

Researcher Jay Michael points out that the Lechuza legend relates to the Mexican word *tecolote* and specifically the Aztec god of death, Mictlantecuhtli, who was often depicted with owls surrounding him.

Native American Legends

We can uncover remarkably similar myths in other parts of North America. For example, in Oklahoma, the Stigini is a six- to nine-foot-tall owlman with putrid flesh hanging from its huge, sharp talons. Its origin can be traced to Indian shaman who take on the form of an animal spirit by killing someone, ripping their heart out, and then burying the organ next to a tree. We must note the similarity of the name Stigini to the word Strigiforme, which indicates the order of birds that includes all owls. Could there conceivably be some European influence woven into these American myths?

From Choctaw and Creek legend, the Ishkitini is an enormous owl that soars through the night sky. It is thought that to hear the Ishkitini shriek is very bad luck, since it is perceived as a warning that death is imminent. The Tlingit people of Alaska's Yakutat region tell of an owlman that fell from a tree and subsequently lived out the duration of its life in Icy Bay until the year 1890. The being's remains were quickly consumed by scavenging crows. But the Yakutat people commemorated the event by erecting a totem adorned with an image of the strange creature.

BIBLIOGRAPHY

Bord, Janet, and Colin Bord. *Alien Animals*. Harrisburg, PA: Stackpole, 1981.

———. *Unexplained Mysteries of the 20th Century*. Chicago: Contemporary, 1989.

Clark, Jerome, and Loren Coleman. *Creatures of the Outer Edge*. New York: Warner, 1978.

Clark, Jerome. *Unexplained!* Detroit: Visible Ink, 1993.

Coffey, Ron. *Kentucky Cryptids: The Search for Kentucky's Hidden Animals*. Kentucky: Fairy Ring, 2010.

Coleman, Loren. *Curious Encounters*. Winchester, MA: Faber and Faber, 1985.

Coleman, Loren. *Mothman and Other Curious Encounters.* New York: Paraview, 2002.

Collins, Andrew. *The Brentford Griffin.* UK: Earthquest, 1985.

Colvin, Andrew B. *The Mothman's Photographer II.* Seattle: Metadisc, 2007.

Downes, Jon. *The Owlman and Others: 30th Anniversary Edition.* Bideford, UK: CFZ, 2006.

Feschino Jr., Frank C. *The Braxton County Monster.* Charleston, WV: Quarrier, 2004.

Freeman, Richard. *The Great Yokai Encyclopedia: A-Z of Japanese Monsters.* Bideford, UK: CFZ, 2010.

Gerhard, Ken. *Big Bird! Modern Sightings of Flying Monsters.* Bideford, UK: CFZ 2007.

Gerhard, Ken, and Nick Redfern. *Monsters of Texas.* Bideford, UK: CFZ, 2010.

Godfrey, Linda S. *Monsters of Wisconsin.* Mechanicsburg, PA: Stackpole, 2011.

Keel, John A. *The Mothman Prophecies.* New York: Signet, 1975.

———. *Strange Creatures from Time and Space.* Greenwich, CT: Fawcett, 1970.

Marlowe, Scott. *The Cryptid Creatures of Florida.* Bideford, UK: CFZ, 2011.

Marshall, Peter. *Mother Leakey and the Bishop: A Ghost Story.* New York: Oxford University Press, 2007.

McCloy, James F. and Ray Miller, Jr. *The Jersey Devil.* Moorestown, NJ: Middle Atlantic, 1976.

McEwan, Graham J. *Mystery Animals of Britain and Ireland.* London: Robert Hale, 1986.

Nunnelly, Barton M. *The Inhumanoids.* Bideford, UK: CFZ, 2011.

Redfern, Nick. *Memoirs of a Monster Hunter: A Five-Year Journey in Search of the Unknown.* Franklin Lakes, NJ: New Page, 2007.

———. *The Real Men in Black.* Pompton Plains, NJ: New Page Books, 2011.

Sergent, Jr., Donnie, and Jeff Wamsley. *Mothman: The Facts Behind the Legend.* Point Pleasant, WV: Mothman Lives, 2002.

Shuker, Dr. Karl P.N. *Dr. Shuker's Casebook.* Bideford, UK: CFZ, 2008.

———. *From Flying Toads to Snakes With Wings.* St. Paul, MN: Llewellyn, 1997.

Steiger, Brad. *Real Monsters: Gruesome Critters, and Beasts from the Darkside.* Detroit: Visible Ink, 2010.

Tralins, Robert. *Supernatural Strangers.* New York: Popular Library, 1970.